ANGELS WEAR BLACK

ANGELS
WEAR
BLACK

CHARLES & NANCY GESCHKE
as told to JO ANN HOFFMAN

CNG PUBLICATIONS
LOS ALTOS, CALIFORNIA

Designed by Lori Barnett
Published by CNG Publications, Los Altos, CA
Printed in the United States of America.
ISBN: 978-0-578-08653-8

First Edition

For our family
present and future

FOREWORD

MANY TIMES over the years I have thought about the four days in May 1992, when I met the Geschke family under the most stressful circumstances imaginable. Even now, nearly twenty years later, memories of that week still provoke strong emotions within me.

My assignment was to be the primary FBI contact for Nan, Kathy, and Peter Geschke, the only family members aware that Chuck Geschke had been kidnapped. As liaison with the FBI's Profiling Unit at the FBI Academy in Quantico, Virginia (now called Behavioral Analysis), I was to provide behavioral assessments on the kidnappers, extracting and interpreting as much information as possible from the ransom calls. I was also responsible for assessing Mr. Geschke—his habits, personality, and likely reactions under stress. What I learned could be critical to the agents in other units responsible for tracking the criminals and locating Mr. Geschke.

When I first arrived at the Geschke home, I didn't know how the family would receive me. Sometimes the mere presence of FBI agents can be extremely upsetting. But despite Nan's understandable suspicion of the agents swarming her home the night before, I needn't have worried. I sensed only their relief that I was there to stay.

My first concern that day was to gain their absolute trust: the next ransom call was expected in a couple of hours, and we had much to get ready. Yet the moment I met Nan, Kathy, and Peter, the pain and fear on their faces nearly overwhelmed me. As they huddled together on the couch facing me, they seemed so vulnerable that for a moment I wished I could simply hug them. However, I could offer only what I hoped were reassuring words about the confidence, competence, and experience of the FBI.

What I didn't mention—and prayed they wouldn't remember—was the case unfolding on the opposite coast that was eerily similar to theirs. Sidney Reso, an Exxon executive, had been kidnapped in front of his New Jersey home the month before. The FBI was still aggressively investigating the case, with no results so far. Thinking about the Reso case could only have broken whatever spirit the Geschkes were clinging to. None of the agents said a word. (Sadly, Sydney Reso's body would be discovered barely a month after Chuck Geschke's safe return.)

During a crisis involving a serious crime, a victim's family will undergo a wide range of emotions, from sadness to denial to anger to guilt: powerful feelings that manifest themselves in random order, often triggered by the slightest detail. I have seen many families implode and disintegrate under a crisis of this magnitude.

Kathy, Peter, and Nan Geschke each endured this emotional roller coaster in his or her own way. But despite the fear, anxiety, and stress that mounted as the days dragged on, this family never argued, never blamed, never even exchanged cross words. Amazingly, they seemed to grow closer as the situation grew bleaker. It was as though they knew intuitively that they must be united to get through this ordeal—an ordeal completely alien to anything they had ever known. An ordeal created by complete strangers. An ordeal from which the possible outcome was terrifying.

This crime was very high risk for the kidnappers—a fact that made Chuck Geschke's safety more tenuous. Their brashness alone was guaranteed to result in a strong and swift law-enforcement response. They abducted a well-known executive with a high profile in the business community. Further, they accosted him in broad daylight from a public parking lot, with a high probability of witnesses. These bold offenders made ransom calls to the family every day—calls that could be both recorded and traced. Their plan to transport the ransom money in a minisubmarine through the waters of Monterey Bay made even a Hollywood movie seem dull. It was clear to the Bureau that Mr. Geschke was, to them, a mere conduit to money. Their type of violence was cold-blooded, goal-directed, and intentional.

In the two decades since the crime, I have worked on hundreds of cases, many of which have silently broken my heart because of the violence and pain inflicted upon the victims and their families. But the Geschke case has always remained particularly significant to me because of the admiration and respect I developed for this unusually close, loving, and resilient family. Reading their story has now allowed me to relive the event and the pain from their perspective. It was a chilling experience.

I would be remiss not to highlight the interactions I had with Kathy Geschke. Our relationship was necessarily the most intense and required the highest levels of trust. We spent many, many hours together preparing for the ransom calls and the money drop. This brave young woman was thrust into a role that would have been daunting for even a seasoned law-enforcement professional, but it was a role she willingly took on for her family, with every reserve of strength she could muster.

The lowest moment for me was putting the bulletproof vest on Kathy to prepare her for the ransom delivery. I was angry that she had to bear this final trauma after all she had dealt with. Unknown even to my colleagues, when Kathy left the house that Friday night, I escaped to another room, closed the door and cried—alone. I had promised her mother and brother that nothing would happen to her—had often reminded them that FBI professionals were literally surrounding her and would protect her with their lives. But now you will know, Nan and Peter, that I feared seeing Kathy leave that night as much as you did.

I have always regretted that when the crisis was over, I never had a chance to say good-bye to Nan, Kathy, or Peter Geschke. So I am honored to be asked to write this Foreword and to finally have the chance to offer a proper tribute and farewell. Being a part of the Geschke family was a privilege. I will not forget that, in them, I witnessed the truest and deepest meanings of faith and family. To all of the Geschkes—and especially to Kathy—my warmest and fondest good wishes.

MARY ELLEN O'TOOLE
FBI Special Agent (retired)
Behavioral Analysis Unit

PREFACE

YEARS AGO, when we first contemplated the idea of writing a book about the ordeal that occurred in May of 1992, we did not know where to start. The event was so fresh and had so enveloped our lives that we became bogged down in trying to fully understand and explain what had occurred.

Now, after several years of telling our story to friends and to community groups, we believe that perhaps writing the story would be beneficial for both us and for readers. So in 2007, we embarked upon writing this book with the help of our dear friend and writer, Jo Ann Hoffman.

We have often given talks about the kidnapping and the effect it has had on our lives and the lives of our children. The centerpiece of those talks has been the realization that it was our faith in God and in each other that allowed us to endure our trial.

After the talks, people would often comment to us that they too had endured some unexpected tragedy, whether it was a death, a divorce, or an illness. They found comfort in hearing our story and how we coped with the trauma. We, in turn, found that we benefited from sharing our story with others.

The events of 1992 continue to impact our lives. We both suffer from post-traumatic stress disorder (PTSD) and will remain on medication for the rest of our lives. The PTSD triggers come much more infrequently now, but they do come—especially for Chuck, who sometimes wakes up in a cold sweat after an awful nightmare.

Because we spent the first month after the kidnapping on Nantucket Island, we now spend our summers there in a community we have come to love and in a home where we can welcome family and friends to a more stress-free environment. Our involvement in the Nantucket community has made us feel just as at home there as in our family residence in Los Altos.

The kidnappers, as of this writing, are still in prison. Once a year, one or both come up for parole hearings, so we are always aware of them. If they are eventually freed on parole*, we expect to feel some anxiety and unease. We cannot tell if the fear we experienced will ever completely leave us, but as the old axiom reminds us, time does heal. So, thankfully, we are not overwhelmed with anxiety these days. Because we have a wonderful family, including seven grandchildren, our lives have been blessed, and that is what we try to concentrate on.

We have been able to recount our story through the generosity of so many people who have helped us with their recollections. Special thanks go to Mary Ellen O'Toole; Dick Held; Ken Thompson; Larry Taylor and Tom LaFreniere, the FBI agents who orchestrated the rescue; our friends Marva and John Warnock; and others who lived this nightmare with us.

We have written this book to tell our story and to communicate our deep belief in the power of prayer and the strength one gets from a strong faith and the loving support of family and friends.

NAN AND CHUCK GESCHKE
August 2010

*In August of 2010 one of the kidnappers was granted parole on condition of deportation. Though this person is no longer in the United States, the anxiety we anticipated has wedged itself into a corner of our minds. We are hopeful that, with the prayers and support of our family and friends, we will be able to keep this uneasiness at bay.

INTRODUCTION

I T WAS 1967. Chuck and Nan Geschke and their two-year-old son, Peter, were living in Cleveland where Chuck was a mathematics instructor at John Carroll University and a doctoral candidate at Case Western Reserve. "All I ever wanted to be was a college math professor," says Chuck Geschke. "And at twenty-seven years old, just a couple years away from my PhD, I thought my career was set for life. But then, something unexpected happened."

It began the day a former student returned to thank Professor Geschke for telling him the hard truth: that he wasn't going to succeed in the graduate math program. As gently as he could, Chuck had ushered the young man out of graduate school, praising his considerable talent, but suggesting a field other than math.

Now, a year later, the student-turned-salesperson was building a bright future selling an exciting new technology for General Electric: computers! To show his gratitude for being steered in a new direction, the student offered to teach Chuck and two of his faculty-member colleagues how to program a computer. Chuck was immediately hooked.

Though powerfully tempted, it seemed irresponsible to Chuck to change his degree program from math to computer science, especially with the advanced degree in math close enough to taste. And there was also his growing family to consider. But his fascination with computers hounded him. He learned that Carnegie Mellon (then Carnegie Tech) in Pittsburgh was, at the time, one of the few universities with a PhD program in computer science.

"Do it," said Nan, the intrepid one, the risk-taker. "Follow your passion. We're young. We're supposed to be exploring things."

So in 1968, with Nan's encouragement and their toddler Peter and new baby daughter Kathleen in tow, Chuck moved the little family to Pittsburgh. Starting over wasn't easy. A fellowship provided Chuck's tuition and a stipend of $350 a month. It wasn't enough. Nan worked from home grading English papers for the school system at two dollars an hour, which added another one hundred dollars a month to the family coffers. When Baby John arrived in 1970, Chuck further supplemented by teaching entry-level programming at a downtown night school. Just so, the Geschkes wearily but happily scraped along until 1972 when Chuck Geschke received his doctoral degree in computer science.

Job opportunities and interviews were plentiful for someone with Chuck's highly specialized degree in an exciting new field. The Xerox Research Center in Palo Alto impressed Chuck the most. After his Xerox interviews, he told his family that he had talked with "the brightest people I ever met." He took the job.

In the fall of 1972, Chuck and Nan sold their little house in Pittsburgh, packed the family car, stowed their seven-year-old, four-year-old, and two-year-old in the backseat, and headed west: to golden California and the fledgling Silicon Valley. The tall, good-looking son of a photo-engraver and homemaker, and the pretty, brown-eyed daughter of a nurse and firefighter, were in high spirits as they set off on the long drive to a new career and a new life.

The trip West made Nan feel like a pioneer. What better adventure for a history buff than to pack up an aging car with three little kids, an odd assortment of possessions, and the bright aura of adventure? She and Chuck were young, eager, educated, and full of optimism about the future awaiting them hundreds of miles across prairie and mountain.

Nan was lonely at first. California was far from the conventional, cautious Midwest where she'd been raised and schooled and had lived and worked. Here at the edge of the continent, the air crackled with possibilities. Excitement about computer technology was palpable. Talent and intelligence radiated from the faces of the men and women she met, most of them engineers and scientists like Chuck, though precious few with young children. Chuck's new colleagues dreamed of the future, talked of it incessantly—lived it.

And here was Nan, wholly immersed in the reality of school buses, Halloween costumes, and potty training. "I'm just a housewife," she would tell Chuck unhappily after every social gathering where intense, arcane conversation sped past her. "Will I ever fit in?"

She needn't have worried. Within a couple of years, Nan took the advice she'd given Chuck to follow the heart. A history major with a passion for research, she'd long been attracted to library science. When five-year-old John entered kindergarten, Nan enrolled in library school part-time at San Jose State University. Four years later and one MLS degree richer, she began building a career as a corporate librarian and research consultant, eventually establishing a library for Westinghouse and becoming president of the Small Libraries Association.

By 1980, Chuck was happily submerged in creative opportunities at Xerox, Nan had achieved a long-term goal of embarking on a career in library science, and the children were thriving with good schools and good friends. Barely eight years after their venturesome cross-country trek, the Geschkes were confirmed and fervent Californians.

The Xerox Research Center of the late '70s was a dream environment for Chuck. Well in advance of most of their competitors and most of the country, Xerox was using personal computers, printers, and even a network to process streams of data. Chuck's innovative ideas and leadership skills were recognized, and he was given the opportunity to form a lab of his own to focus on printing and graphics.

In his search to hire a chief scientist, he interviewed a man he already knew by reputation. Dr. John Warnock and Dr. Charles Geschke were instantly compatible. Both had strong mathematics backgrounds and both had similar philosophies—in business and in life. Both were visionary. They each had two sons and one daughter. "And besides," Chuck says, "we both had beards!"

Shortly after the new Imaging Sciences Laboratory (ISL) was established, Chuck was approached by a Xerox development team charged with designing a set of products that would form the basis of "the office of the future." The team was struggling to define a standard way of communicating between workstations and a variety of laser printers. They asked Chuck if he could assemble a group of researchers to create a printing standard that would satisfy their needs.

Eager to engage in developing this new technology, a team of six computer scientists, including Chuck and John, began developing a protocol for describing the printed page. They code-named it "Interpress." After a little more than a year, Interpress had progressed to the point where Xerox adopted it as a corporate-wide standard to be implemented in all Xerox office computers and printers. ISL had its first major success as a young laboratory.

John and Chuck spent the next several months attempting to persuade the Xerox senior management to begin the process of rolling out a public announcement of Interpress to its customers and the marketplace. To their dismay, Xerox management decided to keep Interpress as proprietary technology for roughly seven years, believing it would take that long to launch the first products and that keeping the technology secret enhanced their competitive advantage.

But John and Chuck instinctively knew that some other high-tech company would recognize the potential of similar technology and push for industry-wide adoption of a competing standard, leaving Interpress behind. Hence, the two began the process of seeking out venture capital to establish a new company to bring a solution to market. Bill Hambrecht, founder of Hambrecht & Quist, enthusiastically agreed to provide the funding to build the new company.

In 1982, with venture capital in place and slightly nervous families behind them, the two left their jobs at Xerox and founded Adobe Systems, naming their company for the creek that flowed behind the Warnocks' home in Los Altos. Then they began to develop their Postscript language for describing the appearance of the printed page. Early interest and subsequent contracts with Apple Computer, Digital Equipment, and Linotype began generating profits for the company by the end of 1983.

Apple's announcement of the Apple LaserWriter in January of 1985 launched the first major printer incorporating Adobe Postscript. Over time, Adobe followed Postscript with an array of broadly adopted technologies and products, such as Adobe Photoshop, Adobe Acrobat, and Adobe Flash, making the company a worldwide leader in digital imaging technologies.

With Adobe's prosperity, the Geschkes' income changed dramatically. Their lifestyle changed as well. But, at the heart of things, Nan and Chuck themselves changed little. "We were still just two runny-nosed kids from Cleveland, Ohio," Chuck says. Little did they know then of the harrowing, life-changing event that lay ahead.

ANGELS WEAR BLACK

The following true story is based on the composite memory of more than a dozen people directly involved in the incident. After nearly twenty years, some blank spots and discrepancies of recall are inevitable, though details have been reconciled as far as possible with the Geschkes' original notes, the FBI files and police interviews from 1992, and the court testimony from 1994.

THE AUTHORS

PROLOGUE

Los Altos, California
Late Friday Night | May 29, 1992

IT'S NEARLY 10:00 PM, and the tree-lined street in old Los Altos is quiet in a friendly, genteel way. A pretty brick and frame colonial spills light from every window, making bars of shadow on the lawn where it crosses the picket fence. A solitary figure, a woman, pauses at an upstairs window, stands motionless and indistinct, then moves away.

At the far end of the house, the garage door rolls open and a knot of people move as one down the few steps from the inside door toward the car: a tall young woman dressed in white; two more women, a little older; and two men. A darker shape hovers in the doorway. The woman from the window? They talk in low voices; there may have been tears. In turn, they cling to the girl, release her, and then grasp her again.

The younger woman is agitated, impatient. She breaks from the little group and returns to the doorway, reaching for the woman in the background. They hold each other in silence with a kind of desperation. Abruptly, the young one turns and runs down the steps, slides behind the wheel of a midnight blue Cadillac, and backs away from the others, down the driveway.

Nan

She's leaving, and I can't stand it. I'm going crazy. They already think I'm crazy, looking all solicitous, insisting that I rest, then insisting that I eat, wanting me to talk, then telling me to stay quiet, checking my

3

prescriptions, whispering when I leave the room. Yes, yes, they love me, they're worried about me, but they're not helping. Nothing helps. Nothing. Well, praying with Peter might help a little.

All I can do tonight is pray and cry. And smoke. I smoke and smoke and smoke. I make up for every year and every minute that I've quit. It's after 10:00. Oh, God. She's leaving. Kathy, my little girl, how I wish it could be me.

I join the rest at the side door to the garage. The money is marked and packed, and the car is wired and ready—ready for my daughter to drive smack into the face of extreme danger. They're checking her gear. I deny to myself that it's a bulletproof vest they're snapping onto my only daughter's chest.

I can't stand to see the fear in her eyes. I can't stand to see her shivering with tension. But there's something else I see in her eyes that heartens me: it's courage, determination, anger, nerve. Strength radiates from this woman-child of mine, washing over all of us. God go with you, Kathy. Please, please come back to us!

• • •

Hollister, California
Early Saturday Morning | May 30, 1992

IT ISN'T A REAL STREET. It's more like a last-minute cutaway that allowed the city of Hollister to pack in a few more houses for a few more tax dollars. Two rows of three small, frame houses, painted a brave yellow, sit doggedly facing one another on the one-hundred-foot strip that turns off a side street at one end. There is no outlet at the other. Hodel Court, it's called.

The occasional street lamps are dim, and the houses, built a scant three feet from the curbside, are mostly closed to the cool darkness this early May morning, doors tight, shades pulled. The blue-white shimmer of a TV screen flickers through the blinds in number 2.

A white-haired woman peers out the front window of number 4, assessing the predawn calm. She's seen a different car this week at number 5. New tenants. Two dark-haired young men, it seems. Not around much ... but lots of fast food going in. She lowers the blinds. They keep their music on too loud, but at least they aren't young rowdies. You never know these days. You're never safe. You barely know who lives next door before they up and move. You just never know. She checks her door lock and turns off the porch light. She wishes she could sleep.

Chuck

By curling my head toward my knees, I am able to raise my cuffed hands enough to inch the blindfold up onto my forehead. I can see, but I still can't stand, even though I worked the leg chains off. There is no way to get leverage, positioned as I am. How can I lift my body over the six-inch-high bolts in the floor?

By purest chance a blanket has been left rolled up near my feet in the corner of the cramped closet. Little by little, I edge it toward me until my hands can pull it over the bolt posts. The resulting cushion, though meager, makes it possible for me to slide my rear end over the bolts and swing my legs out the closet door.

I roll onto my knees, shaking like a beaten dog. With one desperate, heaving motion, I stand. The rest of the chain rains down my legs and puddles at my feet. I'm free! I yank off the blindfold, pull open the bedroom door, and see my shoes near the kitchen wall.

I move fast, heart pounding. Rock has taped a note to the screen door, for Steve, I'm sure, though I can't read Arabic. I step outside. It's liberating to see my surroundings for the first time, even in the dark. They've chosen to hide me in a dreary, nondescript neighborhood, bordering on ramshackle. Of the city or town, I have no idea. And there's no time to speculate. The alley is short and narrow, and only one end leads out. Move, Chuck! Decide! Run!

The predawn dark is soundless. Pale light leaks down the alley from a streetlamp at the corner. I run to the back of the house where I meet with a six-foot wooden fence stretching the length of the alley. The handcuffs prevent me from scaling the fence, but I spy a loose board and try to wrench it down. The sudden noise is loud and grating. Terrified that Rock will hear me and return, I run again to the front and down the alley to the cross street. Which way did Rock go? Which way to safety?

Nagging voices from my past—my high school basketball buddies— flash unbidden through my mind: "Geschke, every play, you run to the right. You're too predictable, man. You never fake anyone out because every darn play you take the ball right. Don't be so predictable, Geschke." I run to the right.

Almost immediately, I see a dark shape running at me, waving his arms like a madman. Though I've never seen his face, I know it's Rock. He's close enough for me to see that one of the wild arms is wielding a knife. Before I can move he's on me, roughing me up, waving the knife, spouting an angry mixture of Arabic and English.

"Why do you do this? Why do you try to get away? You fuck everything up. You stupid fucker! I will kill you." He shoves me forward with the point of the knife between my ribs, and we walk awkwardly back down the alley to the house. There are no lights in the houses. Either no one hears, or no one cares.

Rock is extremely agitated. He pushes me through the door and onto the floor. This time he uses duct tape instead of fabric for the blindfold, pulling it roughly over my eyes. He rebinds my feet with cord and wraps me with the chains—tighter than before—packing me into the miniscule closet like luggage. He turns on the radio and punches up the volume. Then, amidst a shower of verbal threats, Rock leaves once more.

Now in total darkness behind the tape, isolated by noise and distance from anyone or anything rational, I sink into myself. The black poison of despair churns through me, ice cold. I open the door to desolation. I will die. I've seen both their faces now. They can't let me go, even if they get the ransom money. I will die.

From instinct, habit, and years of training at home and school, I turn inward and begin to pray. "It's your ball game now," I tell God. "I want to live, I want to go home, but I guess you have other plans for me. It's 'your will be done,' not mine. Isn't that right, Lord? Help me to accept that. I believe in you. I trust you. Lead me." I lower my head toward my knees and imagine magnificent, invincible arms wrapping around me.

A sense of calm gradually washes over me. I feel its warmth overtaking the desolate chill that had claimed me moments earlier. I breathe more slowly and deeply. All at once I sense a presence—a person! It's Nan. She's truly here, close to me, as real and natural and as fully herself as any day in the twenty-eight years of our life together.

She speaks to me, telling me all will be okay. She'll be fine, the children will be fine. "It's okay, my love. It's okay to leave us," she says over and over. Her voice is soft and tender. But I hear her clearly, and though I can't see or touch her, the sense of her presence is so powerful that I have no doubt she is beside me. I feel cool air brush against my arm.

Then she is gone. I am still afraid, but strangely detached, almost peaceful. Nan has released me. God's arms are around me. I am ready to die.

TUESDAY | MAY 26

· MORNING ·

Nan

I STRETCHED MIGHTILY under the covers and savored the familiar comfort of my own bed. Travel was great, but home was better. Chuck's side of the bed was empty, and I could hear the shower drumming against the tiles of the bathroom. I opened one eye and checked the clock. It was past 7:30—late for me. For another moment or two, I remained deep in the little well of peace surrounding me, mentally reviewing the backlog of phone calls and household business items on my agenda for the day. Maybe I'd stay in my pj's and make my lists until Chuck left for work. Then I could sneak back to bed for a nap after I made the most urgent calls. Might take a few lazy days to wipe out four weeks of cumulative jet lag. I got up and went downstairs to make coffee.

"Why didn't you sleep in?" Chuck asked when he came into the kitchen a few minutes later. He sounded annoyed, but as usual, he looked crisp and appealing. Chuck was a presence. Tall and broad-shouldered with a strong, square, competitive set to his jaw beneath a slightly graying beard, Chuck could be intimidating—but only for about thirty seconds. Kind blue eyes, a genial smile, and a ready wit usually gave him away. I didn't get any indulgent smiles this morning, however.

"You're going to be a wreck all week if you don't get more sleep," he said, pouring himself some coffee. "I still think going to Russia was crazy after just getting back from Europe."

I was weary of arguing about the Russia decision. We'd wrung every drop of water out of that rag. I wasn't going to admit it—yet—but Chuck was probably right. On the long trip home last Friday, I had been tightly wound with both fatigue and impatience to dig into the packed schedule of the coming week. I finally snapped at a flight attendant and made a stupid scene over some ridiculous issue, embarrassing myself and my travel group. I had felt like a limp balloon the next day, ashamed of my ugly disposition.

"I'll go back to bed if I can," I said. "I need to get a few things done first. Will you call me as soon as you get to work and check your calendar? I need to get the plane tickets confirmed for New Jersey and then for Nantucket, too."

"Sure," he said, folding the newspaper on the counter and heading for the back door. "I'm going to pick up the croquet wickets we left in the yard yesterday. I'm sure the lawn guys will appreciate it." He grinned. "Lots of fun to cross a wicket with a mower, huh? Be right back."

A little after 8:00, the phone rang. Janice Coley, Chuck's administrative assistant, wanted to catch Chuck before he left for the office. He could skip the suit and tie today, she said. No outside visitors or client meetings. I promised to pass the word to Chuck. Longtime friends, Janice and I chatted a few minutes about my recent trip and Kathy's graduation party yesterday.

When Chuck came back inside, I gave him the message and he hustled upstairs to change. I poured more coffee and reached for the phone. I was punching in the numbers for the travel agency when Chuck left about twenty to nine. Our travel agent put me on hold while she searched for flight options. I leaned against the kitchen counter and let my gaze roam through the window and across the yard, holding the phone in one hand and my coffee in the other.

John's graduation June 9 was the next big circle on the family calendar. Only two weeks from now, and I still didn't have our times and tickets locked down. The family Nantucket vacation was just a week later. Despite the crunch of events and looming deadlines, I was happy. Two college graduations within two weeks, and Peter's wedding at the end of the summer to his darling Diane. Our first wedding! A memory triggered and I jotted a note to call the dressmaker. My mother-of-the-groom dress would be ready for a fitting this week. Hope I didn't gain any weight in Russia. I stood up straight and practiced pulling in my stomach muscles.

Was it already twenty years since Chuck and I had made that first hesitant trek across the country from Pittsburgh to Palo Alto with three little ones, almost no money, and even less sophistication? Chuck and Nan—just two ordinary kids from Cleveland, Ohio, with a sense of adventure and giddy optimism about this weird new field of computer science. I almost laughed out loud remembering. I loved those kids we were. That's who we still are, I thought, and always will be.

I was still smiling when Kathleen returned to the phone. I took down the flight options and promised to call her back as soon as Chuck checked in with his calendar.

◆ ◆ ◆

Chuck

I WAS GLAD today would be laid-back at the office. I felt like I was still on a treadmill from our trips, the graduation, the parties. Good things, true, but I was tired. And it wouldn't be a restful week. It was the last week of the quarter, so we'd be preoccupied with results. I tossed my briefcase onto the passenger seat of my new, dark green

Mercedes 500, still getting a minor kick out of owning the sporty vehicle. Like a kid, I thought, smiling a little.

I pulled out of the shady pathway beside our Los Altos home and headed down University Avenue for the twenty-minute drive to Adobe Systems headquarters in Mountain View. It was only a quarter to nine and already a gorgeous day. I merged into traffic seamlessly.

Things should settle down now. Nan was back from Russia, Kathy was duly graduated from USF, the Memorial Day barbecue was a great family time, and, thank God, we didn't have any special events until John's graduation. After that, vacation on the East Coast. Then nothing for weeks until Peter's wedding in mid-August. No question that would be the major event of the summer for us.

Traffic was light and I felt some of my weariness fade into the hypnotic hum of the powerful engine. I'd been annoyed with Nan this morning. She was obviously exhausted, and I felt bad for her. But she never seemed to stop going and doing, even when it was too much for her—for anyone, really. The trip to Russia had put me over the top. I didn't want her to go. She shouldn't have gone, and she knew it. Yeah, it *was* a great opportunity for her video work—and she was passionate about the historical video programs she was doing through her work with the Historical Commission. That part I understood.

But her judgment was flawed this time. She'd had surgery in March, we'd gone to Europe for two weeks in April, and two weeks later she was off to Russia for a week. Then Kathy's graduation and a weekend of parties began the day after she returned. She had to be dog-tired. No wonder she was on edge. Why did she do this to herself? To me? The stress she couldn't handle always seemed to land on my shoulders. I squelched a nugget of resentment and resolved to call Nan from work and tell her to stay in bed all day if she wanted to. Get herself thoroughly rested and back to our normal routine.

I turned into the parking lot off Charleston Road and swung into my usual spot beside the entry to Building C. I was anxious to meet with Janice and get a handle on the morning's agenda. I pulled my briefcase from the car and swung the door shut just as a light gray Ford Taurus stopped behind and perpendicular to the Mercedes. A compact, dark-haired young man jumped from the rear door and came toward me with a map in his hand.

"Do you work here?" the man asked.

"Yes, I do. Can I help you find something?" In the maze of office buildings that lined Charleston Road, it was common to find strangers asking directions. Happy to help, I walked toward the man.

When I was about three feet away, the man lifted the map slightly to reveal the long, dark-metal barrel of a gun pointing directly at my heart. "You're coming with me," he said. He stepped forward and gripped my forearm like a vise, pushed the gun into my rib cage, and steered me toward the backseat of the running car.

I couldn't comprehend what was happening. Was this some kind of prank? Was this a real gun? I glanced toward the door of my building no more than fifty feet away. No faces or voices. I was surrounded by the five buildings belonging to Adobe and filled at this hour with hundreds of employees, yet I didn't see or hear a soul. I was completely alone—and scared out of my wits.

"You're being kidnapped," he said. "Get in, get in. Do what I tell you." With a gun only inches from every vital organ I possessed, I complied. With his final shove, I stumbled into the backseat.

The man slid in beside me and slammed the door. "Let's go," he said to the driver.

This must be what terror is. I'm shaking. I'm confused. My heart is racing. I'm in total disbelief. I can think only of the small circle of flesh between my ribs where the nose of the gun is jammed against me. This is not a joke, I tell myself. This is real. This is real. Like a flash of light on the psychedelic screen of my brain, I suddenly remember the sensational kidnapping of an Exxon executive in New Jersey about a month ago. They hadn't found him yet. The car sweeps off on the swelling wave of my panic.

・ ・ ・

Nan

I GLANCED at the kitchen clock. After nine and Chuck hadn't called.
Darn. Someone probably cornered him with a problem before he got
to his office. I called Janice and asked her to interrupt him briefly and
remind him to check his calendar for our New Jersey trip.

"I haven't seen him come in yet, Nan," she said.

"That's strange. He left a half hour ago," I said.

"I could page him for you," Janice offered. "Once in a while he goes
to another building to chat with the engineers. Still, he usually lets
me know where he is."

"Don't bother paging him. He has to be somewhere close by. I'll
call back in a few minutes."

I made a few more calls. One of the first was an apology to Heidi,
our Russia trip coordinator, for the unfortunate incident on the plane.
She brushed the whole thing off with kind words, and we compared
notes on what stress and fatigue can do to a person. Heidi even shared
a few classic stories of her own. I was immensely reassured.

Next, a quick call to confirm that I hadn't forgotten about the
cake I promised to deliver for the cheese co-op dinner tonight. Then,
adopting Chuck's logic about the Russia trip, I called my Red Cross
committee chair and reluctantly canceled my reservation for the upcoming convention in Baltimore. I knew I had hit the wall with my
summer schedule. Something had to go.

With the priority calls out of the way, I went upstairs to finish
unpacking and start the laundry. Our housekeeper, Cely, let herself
in and met me on her way to the laundry room. She'd be busy reor-
ganizing the house today after all the company last night. As I was
beginning to feel that my day was on track, it struck me that Chuck
hadn't called yet. Odd. He was punctual and meticulous about doing

what he promised—almost obsessive about it. I called the office again. It was nearly 10:00.

"He still hasn't checked in, Nan. John Warnock hasn't seen him yet either, though one of the employees told us his car was in the parking lot as usual." Janice told me she'd paged him twice to no avail and was a little concerned. "This is not like Chuck at all," she said.

I felt my breath catch slightly at the back of my throat. A little bump of anxiety. "Maybe he's sick somewhere," I said. A heart attack? I willed myself to be calm. "Will you page him again, Janice?"

"Not only that, Nan," she said with characteristic resolve, "but I'll physically check all five buildings myself, including the restrooms. And his car."

I abandoned any thought of a nap, took a quick shower, and began to get dressed. Surely Janice or John would call back in a few minutes with a perfectly reasonable explanation for this lapse on the part of my always predictable, always dependable husband.

I tried to be patient. I finished dressing and tidied up the bedroom. I wanted to give Janice enough time to do a thorough search of the property before I called back. To distract myself, I called Kathy about her plans for the Nantucket trip. We talked about the house we were renting, the clothes we'd need—comfortable girl talk. About 11:00, I checked in with my committee for the TV documentary and reminded everyone of our edit session at the Foothills College studio at 6:00 that evening.

Cely and I worked side by side for a while picking up stray glasses and other leftovers from last night's barbecue. By 11:30, neither Chuck nor Janice had called. I was sick with worry. A fluttering chill rooted in the pit of my stomach and was gradually rising to my throat. Something was drastically wrong. I was sure of it.

I called Janice. "Nothing, Nan. Nothing," she said. "I searched every building myself and also looked through his car windows from every angle. His sunglasses are there, but his briefcase isn't." Her voice trembled slightly. "I can't explain it, Nan. Neither can John. I know you're worried by now. We are too. What could have happened?"

"You looked in all the bathrooms? Even the toilet stalls? What if he's fallen unconscious somewhere? What if he's hurt, Janice? Are you sure you covered every possible room?" I could hear my voice pitching higher, but I couldn't help it.

"I'm sure. I don't know what else to do."

I breathed deeply—once, twice—and stayed quiet for a minute. When I spoke, I sounded calmer than I felt. "I'll come in and talk to John." I decided only as I said it. "We'll figure out what to do next." Act. We had to act. Check the freeway accident reports. Check the hospital emergency rooms. Call the police.

My decisiveness both surprised and energized me. Before I left, I called Kathy again. My strong, sensible daughter had shoulders broad enough for the entire family. And how often we leaned on them! It was instinctive to let Kathy know what was going on.

"Okay, so it's a bit out of character for Dad to go AWOL on us," she said. "But you know how he can get really absorbed in something to the point of blocking everything out."

Yes, I did know that.

"Well, then. He'll eventually get hungry or thirsty or something and realize the time and then be all mortified that he made everybody worry." I heard the slow smile in her voice. "He'll fall all over himself apologizing."

I sighed and managed a small laugh. "You're probably right. I'll call you as soon as I hear from him. Thanks, Kath. And don't forget to block out your vacation dates for Nantucket." Encouraged and determined, I grabbed my purse and keys and told Cely I'd be gone for a while. The phone rang as I headed for the door.

"About time," I muttered, and turned back to answer, certain it was Janice, or Chuck himself, and already tasting relief. I grabbed the receiver from the kitchen counter.

• • •

Chuck

I COULD SEE the driver only from behind, but he appeared to be short, slender, and dark like his partner, though more muscular. My first irrational thought was, "They're Russians." Fear had knee-jerked me back to the "red" threats of my college days in the sixties. But no, these guys were trim and dark complected, with thick black hair. Arabic, maybe? Middle Eastern?

As we took off from the parking lot, the man again nudged my ribs with the gun and told me in clear, slightly accented English, "You can call me Steve." Inclining his head toward the driver, Steve said, "He's Rock."

Steve continued with a certain formality, as though the situation was rehearsed. "You are going to be held for ransom. We know you have money and your family will pay. Then we will send you to our people in Lebanon. The organization, the big organization, will get even more ransom. There is a plan for you."

I began to shake despite the California sun streaming through the car windows. "My family, please don't hurt my family. We'll pay whatever you want. Just don't hurt them."

"We won't if they don't do anything stupid," he said, an acid edge in his voice. "Stop looking at me. Look down. Look away."

He sounded angry so I closed my eyes. I heard a tearing sound and felt him press a circle of tape to each eye. I had seen him fingering a soda can with two circular patches of gray duct tape fixed to it. My blindfold. I should have guessed. He pushed the tape firmly against the skin around my eyes. I could see nothing except variations of gray—the hazy convergence of light and dark. Then I felt glasses being hooked behind my ears, and I recalled seeing sunglasses on the seat. Clever. No one would be able to tell I was blindfolded.

With blindness, however, all of my remaining senses sharpened.

There was a faint smell of some spice or seasoning I couldn't identify. That odor clashed with the cloying, distinctive fragrance of rental car deodorizer. One of the men—Rock—made a constant sniffing sound. Were they on cocaine? Maybe they wanted money for drugs. Would they kill me for that? Only that? I strained to make my mind work, to make sense of things.

Traffic sounds increased, noisy trucks, higher speeds. I guessed we had merged onto the freeway. It would have to be the 101, given the turns we took and the short length of time from the Adobe parking lot. The sun had moved a little higher on my left shoulder, now beginning to warm my neck and ear—confirmation that we were going south. South on 101, I repeated to myself. I was desperate to remember and had an absurd wish for a notebook. The first moment I got away, I would need to tell everyone where to find me. I clung to each bit of information as though it were a stout, seaworthy log that would keep me from drowning.

"Want to chain him up?" Rock shot the question over his shoulder to Steve, jolting me back to the moment.

"Nah, he'll be fine." Steve turned to me. "But don't try anything, don't try to get away." He pushed the gun tighter into my ribs for emphasis.

"I won't resist anyone with a gun," I told him.

"Good. That's smart. Just remember to cooperate. Your family has to cooperate. If they don't, if they do something stupid or if you do something stupid, we will blow up your house. We know where you live. Right now there's a bomb planted in your front yard. Nitroglycerine. If you don't cooperate, we push a button and *bam!* Your house and your neighbors' houses are gone—like that." He snapped his fingers. Rock's brother was an expert on explosives, he told me. I believed him.

My God, Nan is there, she's home. They'll hurt her, they'll kill her ... God, do you hear me? Spots race before my blinded eyes,

20

colliding and exploding in pinpricks of light. I feel faint and sick.
What can I do? How can I warn her? Who will help me? Please,
God. Protect her. Protect my children.

Suddenly, Steve demanded, "Give me your wallet." He pulled the gun back a little to give me room to maneuver. Envisioning the gun now just inches from my eyes as I bent forward, I pulled the wallet from my back pocket. Again, fear rose into my throat like vomit. The credit cards and cash meant nothing. Exposing my list of the names and addresses of my children terrified me. To distract him, I gave him my side wallet too, without prompting.

They found several $100 bills and lesser denominations that may have totaled $1,200 or $1,300. The money interested them. "You got lots of money. You're a wealthy man," Rock said almost softly, as though savoring the sound of the words. Then loudly, suddenly, "How much did you pay for that car?" He referred to my Mercedes.

Since the car was a recent purchase, I clearly remembered negotiating the price and answered honestly. "About $90,000."

"You're lying. You're a fuckin' liar," Rock spat out from the front seat. "You paid $127,000 for that car, and you know it. You start lying to us, you'll pay and your family will pay."

At the mention of my family, the white heat of fear overtook me again. I kept silent as the car slowed, and I swayed with the curve of an exit ramp. From the position of the sun, I figured we'd been traveling about thirty minutes. I struggled to picture a map and the names of towns thirty to forty miles down Highway 101 from Mountain View. My mind's eye was as blind as my real ones. There were dozens and dozens of nondescript farming towns along this corridor. I couldn't come up with the name of a single one.

We made a left turn, and I heard the muted sound of freeway traffic above us. We were beneath the overpass. Then a quick right turn. The crunch of gravel under the tires about three minutes later suggested a side road or driveway. We slowed to a crawl.

"We'll stay here for a little while, and then we go to the 'safe house' until your wife gets the money," said Steve. He added menace to his voice. "If she won't cooperate, or if you do something stupid, we will cut you into little pieces and feed you to the sharks. They will never find you. Not even a piece of you. Ever." Another jab of the gun to my ribs.

We stopped completely, and Steve reached across me to unlock the car door. My heart began to race again, and my breath came in shallow gulps. They pulled me out of the car into bright sunlight. My eyes burned behind the tape.

"Start walking and don't speak," Steve directed. He took my arm and kept the gun tight against my ribs. We took only a few steps before I heard the sound of a key turning in a lock. He pushed me forward, and the light was blotted out. The smell of old dust and damp carpet was overpowering. I had no doubt we were in a cheap motel room.

They sat me in a chair that creaked under my weight like plastic or vinyl. I could sense Steve's shadow looming directly over me. Then he sat and leaned toward me. His voice was so close, I could feel the soft explosion of his consonants on my face. Based on the pitch of the occasional comments made by Rock, I guessed he was across the room.

"Now we talk about money," Steve began. "And we want the truth from you. Understand?"

"Yes, yes."

He raised his voice. "If you value your life, if you value your family's lives, you will tell the truth. No lies. Understand?"

I smelled the faint mustiness of spices on his breath. "Yes! I understand." I spoke loudly, trying hard to mask my fright. I hoped I was convincing.

"Good," said Steve. "Because Rock here, he's a touchy one. Don't spook him with any lies. He gets spooked, he takes people out. Makes shark bait out of 'em. Just cuts 'em up and throws 'em in the ocean. Done it plenty of times—right, Rock?"

"Yeah. Ready to do it again," Rock growled.

"Uh, I—ah ... okay." I tried to sound submissive this time.

"You got lots of money. How much?"

"Well, I don't—"

"No lies!" Steve shouted. "We'll know if you lie."

How much information did they have? I suddenly remembered that the *San Jose Mercury News* had published its annual list of salaries for Silicon Valley executives a few days ago. Shit. These guys had company information dropped in their laps. I couldn't risk giving them bogus numbers.

"I honestly can't say for sure how much I have. Most of it's in company stock. And that value changes every day." I hoped they understood that stock options or shares didn't mean cash in your pocket. As emphatically as I could, I added, "That's the truth."

"Then guess how much." I heard a *klunk* on the table where I figured Steve was sitting. He must have put the gun down to remind me he still had it.

"I guess about fifteen or sixteen million dollars," I said, trying to estimate an average stock price times my approximate number of shares.

"Tell us how to get it," Steve demanded.

"Well, the government has all kinds of regulations on selling that stock, you know. So the money isn't really available to me."

"There's other money," Rock snapped from his post across the room. "Tell us what else."

"Any other investments would probably take about ten days to convert into cash," I said. "But I have some bank accounts that might convert faster. Maybe we could get three or four hundred thousand together in a couple of days." I strained to sense a reaction from either of them. Nothing audible but the sounds of Steve shuffling and stacking my credit cards and bank cards on a tabletop. And Rock's ubiquitous sniffing. They talked to each other in Arabic.

Abruptly, they began asking questions about the kids. Who's Kathy? Peter? John?

23

I felt a chill and began trembling, realizing they had found the card with the kids' addresses. "They don't have anything to do with this. They don't have money … they can't—" My voice got stronger, angry at the potential threat to my children.

"Shut up!" Rock yelled.

"We know about them already," Steve said calmly. "We want to be sure you are telling us the truth. Now tell us about them."

I took a deep breath. "Uh … Peter's a math teacher, junior high, lives in Fremont, and Kathy, my daughter, she lives in San Francisco and is looking for a job." I stopped. Let them assume I was finished. That should be enough to prove I wasn't lying. John wasn't in California. Maybe I could still protect him.

"John." Steve prompted. "Who is John?"

"My other son, the younger one," I answered dully. "He's in college in New—"

"You're a Jew, aren't you?" Rock cut me off with a baffling change of direction.

The fear sitting on my chest rose to my throat. "No."

"You are. Geschke is a Jewish name." Rock sounded annoyed, as if he badly wanted me to be Jewish.

"It's a German name. I'm Catholic."

"Tell the truth." Rock raised his voice, came close to my chair, and apparently picked up the gun. I felt the barrel in the center of my chest.

"Remember the bomb. If you lie, we will detonate the bomb," added Steve.

"I'm telling you the truth, dammit!" They must have sensed my desperation because, again, they abruptly changed gears.

"Okay. Time to kick back," Steve said. They turned on the TV and began to search the channels for a movie, ignoring me.

After a time, I began to breathe more evenly, but still alternated between feeling occasional chills and the beading of sweat on my face. I lost any sense of sunlight in the dimness of the room, so I couldn't gauge the time. I figured it had been at least two hours since we left my car in the Adobe lot. My mind was still clogged with disbelief and fear. I struggled to think of options, of some action I could take, but the thought of the promised violence to Nan and the children paralyzed me.

I sat quietly, afraid that any movement on my part could get me killed. I listened while my captors talked casually for maybe an hour about cars and TV shows and money—but mostly cars. The best kinds. The most expensive kinds. The ones they dreamed of. The ones they would buy when they got the ransom money. It must have been around noon when I heard Steve stand and stretch.

"Time to call your wife about the money." He leaned in close to me. In a low voice meant to sound like he was my buddy, Steve reminded me that Rock was volatile. "Be sure you do whatever he says. He'll go crazy if you don't," Steve said. "If you don't cooperate, you'll be shark bait. Little pieces of you all over the ocean." For about the fifth time, I got the message.

The door closed and the car started. The only sounds left were the low hum of the TV voice track, Rock's constant sniffling, and the menacing metallic click of the hammer on the handgun that Rock was pulling back and letting go in a sinister rhythm.

Nan, I hope you're not home. I don't want you and the kids drawn into this—whatever it is. But I need you. I'm scared out of my wits. Please just get the money, any amount of money. They're serious, Nan. I hope you can stay calm. Get the kids to come. Don't call the police! But my God, you need the police! My life is in your hands, Nan. All our lives. Why is this happening to us? Have to pray. You've got to get us out of this, God. Mary, Mother of God, help us. Remember O most gracious Virgin Mary that never was it known that …

• • •

Nan

BEFORE I COULD say hello, a male voice said, "Mrs. Geschke?"

"Yes. Who's call—"

"Are you listening?"

"Yes." I struggled to think who we knew that would begin a conversation in this way. It struck me as odd, but he did seem to know me, and he did pronounce our name correctly, so—

"Your husband has been kidnapped, and he's been transported out of state. And—are you listening to me?" The voice became terse and demanding.

"Yes, I'm listening to you." My voice was a dry whisper. The familiar kitchen surroundings fell into a white fog. My vision blurred. I closed my eyes and gripped the phone until my knuckles turned white and the veins on the back of my hand grew rigid.

"We want $650,000 in $100 bills. Do you understand?"

"I—no, I don't understand." My voice sounded so faint to my own ears that I hoped he could hear me.

His voice became strident, angry. "Why? Are you stupid?"

"I don't understand what you mean!" I prayed I wouldn't cry.

"Why? Aren't you listening? You're rich. You can get the money somewhere—call your bank, clean out your checking accounts. We know you can get the money. If you don't, you'll find your husband cut up in pieces on your front doorstep."

My breathing became rapid and raw. It sounded noisy from the echoing space I was inhabiting between the telephone receiver and my mind. I was vaguely aware that Cely had left her position at the sink and was moving toward me in the kitchen bay, surely puzzled by my strange behavior.

"Are you there? Are you listening?" The caller was nearly shouting

26

now. "Don't dare to call the police. Don't let anyone know about this call. We are watching you. We know where you live. If you contact anyone at all, your husband will be executed."

I couldn't speak. I could barely breathe. I turned away from the anxious Cely and walked into the den beside the breakfast room.

He continued, faster, as if he were irritated and anxious to be finished. "Next, you will get your husband's car from the parking lot."

"Okay. Okay. Where do I take it?" My voice was shaking. I only wanted him to know that I would do anything he asked, anything to get my husband back safely.

"Have the car out of there by 5:00 PM. Take it home. Do you understand?"

"No, I don't understand anything. But I'll do what you want." I was crying by now. "Whatever you want. What do—"

"Shut up! Just shut up and listen to me. If that car is not gone by five o'clock, we will feed your husband to the sharks. Are you listening?"

"Yes, yes, I'm listening, yes."

"I'll call you back in two days. You have ten days to get the money."

"Yes, okay, yes."

"Do you understand? Answer me!"

"I understand. Yes, okay. I—"

He hung up.

Dear God, what is happening? I am trembling and very cold. I walk into the dining room without a word to Cely and sit stiffly in the formal, high-backed chair, trying to compose myself. I will not fall apart. Help me, Lord. Help me to stay calm. My Chuck, my love, where are you? Who has you? Are you hurt? Are you scared? Who will help us? I can't call the police. They're watching! They'll know! Oh, God, help us. I can't do this alone. But I have to—with you, Lord, I promise I'll help you, Chuck. If God helps me. Oh, dear God!

I told Cely to leave for the rest of the day. I saw the hurt and confusion in her eyes, but I had to protect her. And I needed to think, to make a plan. She was close to tears as she closed the door softly behind her. Alone and heart pounding, I searched for Chuck's keys. I'd never driven the Mercedes and didn't know where he kept his extra set, but thankfully, I found them in his top dresser drawer. I left for Adobe to get the car.

My mind was racing. Should I talk to Janice or John? Should I ask … who would … John, yes. John Warnock would know what to do. He and Chuck were not only business partners, but close and loyal friends. The thought of talking with John and Marva Warnock comforted me. I trusted them completely. Then a thought pricked at me like a needle. John! John could be a target, too! Were they watching Adobe? I had to warn him immediately that he might be in danger.

I needed a safe phone. I stopped at our dry cleaners. The car behind me stopped too, but no one got out. Had they been following me? I went inside to the counter, and a woman came in at my heels. Was she one of them? I began shaking again. No, I wouldn't make a phone call here. They would know. *Oh my God, I'm being followed by people with guns and knives.* I had never felt so vulnerable. Wherever I went, I was dragging danger in my wake.

I returned to the car and started to circle through town. I would make it seem like I was doing my regular errands. That might confuse whoever was following me. A local woman doing household errands should be able to fade into the street traffic. Maybe if I stopped at the library, I could use the phone to get a message to John.

The Mountain View library was on a side street, not easily visible from the main downtown streets. Familiar with the town, I wove around several small streets and came up behind the building. As a librarian myself, I had friends on the library staff. My friend Kent must have sensed my tension when, without any of our usual small talk, I said I had urgent need of a phone. With a solemn glance, but without any questions, he led me to a private office.

My fingers were trembling as I pressed the numbers. "Janice?" I prayed my voice wasn't wavering. I didn't want Janice to ask any questions. Her familiar, caring voice might cause me to lose my fragile control.

"Nan—have you heard from Chuck? We're all worried to death here. We—"

I broke in and blurted, "Janice, will you give John a message for me?"

"Well, sure, of course. But we—"

"Tell him to meet me at the Rancho Market in Los Altos at 3:30."

"But why do you—"

"I can't talk now. Just please give him the message. It's very important. It's critical." I pressed my lips together to keep my teeth from chattering. I had to get off the phone before I broke down.

"Okay, I will. Are you all right, Nan? You sound funny."

"I have to go, Janice." I hung up and suppressed a sob. I felt completely disconnected from my former life.

I left from the front door of the library and walked down the street toward town. In a minute, I would circle around the building to my car in the rear lot. I felt the eyes of my librarian friends tracing question marks on my back. Usually we had long, lively conversations about new books, new research techniques, new media resources— the things that united us in loving libraries almost as much as we loved our children. They had to be confused by my remoteness, my reluctance to even meet their eyes.

If only they knew. If only my problem could be resolved by looking up the appropriate reference book. Something like: *Six Ways to Respond to a Kidnapper Who Has Your Husband—Without Being Terrified.* On the edge of hysteria, I made an eerie, desperate sound that was part laugh, part scream, and part anguished cry.

· AFTERNOON ·

Nan

FROM THE LIBRARY, I drove to Adobe to exchange cars. I was clutching the wheel in both hands, my shoulders hunched forward. I told myself, without much success, to breathe deeply. Just before I turned onto Charleston Road a few blocks away from Adobe, a sudden *pop-crack!* exploded on my left, breaking into the quiet afternoon.

I jerked the wheel involuntarily, almost hitting the curb. I accelerated the car as my heart thumped crazily. When the hush of the afternoon closed in around me again in a matter of seconds, I realized that a car in the opposite lane had backfired. Nothing more. Any other day, I might have laughed at my panic, but not this day. Gunfire was within my reality now.

At 1:30 in the afternoon, the Adobe Systems parking lot was packed with cars, but empty of people—thankfully. I swung into the spot next to Chuck's car. As I started to get out, I saw a familiar figure crossing from her car to the office door. Was it Ann Robinson? A friend and loyal staffer, Ann and I regularly worked together to plan employee social events.

Thank God she hadn't noticed me. I couldn't possibly talk to anyone. I ducked back inside the car and bent my head. After a couple of minutes, keeping my head down, I slid into Chuck's car, praying that I could figure out all the fancy knobs and dials. There wasn't a human being in sight when I slowly rolled out of the parking lot.

Purposely twisting and turning onto side streets through Mountain View and Los Altos, I returned home. Once inside, I set the security system but didn't feel any safer. I changed into some lightweight sweats for walking and then got down to business.

I wrote a note to John Warnock, explaining what had happened to Chuck and warning him that he could be next. "Don't come to the house," I told him. "They're watching." I asked him to meet me sometime after 6:00 that evening in the TV studio at Foothills College where I'd be working with my committee on a documentary. Then we could decide what to do. I ended with, "Whatever you do, don't call the police. Chuck would be killed!"

The money. That was next. Terrified that someone might see me using the phone, I crab-crawled under the kitchen window that faced the street and went to our lower-level office to call the brokers. On the first call, to our San Francisco investment firm, I was routed to voice mail. The familiar taped voice of our broker's assistant comforted me. Kay was a person I had long liked and trusted. My eyes filled. When the message tone beeped, I blurted out that Chuck had been kidnapped and that we needed money immediately.

Even before I disconnected, I realized what I had done. I had *told!* And I had told on our *home phone!* What was I doing? What had I done? If the phone was tapped, they would know I had exposed the crime. *Forgive me, Chuck!*

Shaking now, I dialed our other broker at Alex Brown. When John Kryzanowski began a familiar and friendly conversation at the other end of the line, I cut him off. "John, I can't talk right now. I need $650,000 in cash—all in $100 bills," I said, "and I need it immediately. Just let me know how much we can get and when you can have it to me. Thank you." I could only imagine how formal and stiff I sounded. John Kryzanowski, who knew us well, was sure to be puzzled.

It was past 2:30. I'd just have time to cover the two and a half miles to Rancho Market to meet John Warnock at 3:30. Folding the note inside my bra, I left through the garage. As I pulled open the door, the alarm screeched in protest. I yelped in surprise and immediate fear, then remembered that I had the system turned on while I was inside. I punched in the code and reset the alarm to leave. I stood outside the garage door for a minute trying to slow my breathing.

"Mrs. Geschke?"

"Uh! Oh!" I backed away as our gardener, Forrest, came toward me, brandishing his long-barreled leaf blower.

"Did you need us to do anything special today, Mrs. Geschke?" he asked.

"Uh, no. Nothing special, Forrest. I just don't want anyone in the front yard. Work in the backyard only, please." I eyed the team of workers and cache of tools behind him and was overwhelmed with suspicion. The blade of the hedge-trimmer was long and sharp. The shovels looked heavy, with thick wooden handles. Even a rake could be a weapon. I knew I was being irrational, but I couldn't help it.

I edged past them. "We're having company on the patio tonight, so we need everything done in the back. No work in the front yard today," I repeated, backing away as I spoke.

Clearly baffled, they nodded assent. "Yes, ma'am."

The day was unusually hot for May. Nearly ninety degrees. I walked fast and was soon perspiring heavily. Despite the discomfort, I was glad to be on foot. The kidnappers might have known our cars, but they might not have known what I looked like. I had a better chance of becoming anonymous this way.

It was already 3:30 by the time I reached Rancho. Trying to act casual, I got a grocery cart and, on shaky legs, began to travel the aisles, stopping now and then to stare blankly at the rows of cans and boxes before me.

As I turned the corner to the cereal aisle, I saw John Warnock pushing a basket in my direction. He started to call my name, but I didn't look at him. Instead, I picked up speed and passed him, barely pausing to pass him the note I had pulled from my shirt. He didn't try to follow as I fled toward the meat counter.

Back outside, I leaned against the brick wall on the side of the building and pulled a Coke from the few grocery items I had picked up. I was weak, flushed, and still had more than two miles to walk back home in punishing heat. The cold drink helped. I began my trek.

Near the end of the Rancho parking lot, I passed the camera shop. I'd been in there so often before the Russia trip that one of the employees had become my friend as well as my film mentor. I went in.

"Pete, can you drive me home?" I said by way of greeting. "I'm really tired, and I don't have my car."

He looked upset. "Oh, I would in a minute, Nan. I hope you know that. But I'm the only one here today. I can't leave the store."

I suddenly felt foolish. "No, no, I understand. Don't even think of it. I'm fine. Really." I gave him what I hoped was a smile and left quickly. I wanted to cry, but the shell I had built to keep myself together wouldn't crack. I would handle this myself. Every person I loved depended on it. *But it's too much weight for me!*

I kept a good pace down the boulevard and was turning onto University Avenue when a car pulled up behind me and honked lightly. Instinctively, without looking back, I began to run.

"Nan, wait!"

The voice calling after me was familiar. I stopped and turned around. It was Pete.

"Please let me take you the rest of the way," he said. "You looked so worried and tired that I decided to close the shop and come after you. Come on, Nan. Get in."

I gratefully accepted the ride for the remaining few blocks to the house, thanked Pete, and went around back to go inside. One of the gardeners stopped me.

"The police were here, Mrs. Geschke," he said.

I had a moment of wild confusion. "Police? Here? What do you mean?"

"Came about the alarm," he said. His look was reproachful and guarded, as if I had mistrusted them and called the police.

Then it clicked. I had not called the security company when I left the house to tell them the alarm had tripped accidentally. Of course the police would have come by to check the property. I apologized and explained awkwardly to the yard crew.

In a haze of disbelief, I let myself in, armed the system again and slowly slid my back down the wall to sit in a heap on the floor.

Things are unraveling. Look what I've done! Police have been crawling around our grounds in plain sight. And besides that, I told about the kidnappers on a voice mail! I've done exactly what the kidnappers told me not to do! Oh, Chuck, I've been so careful, I'm trying so hard, and look how I've botched things. Dear God, take care of Chuck. Help me to help him.

• • •

Chuck

EMOTIONALLY DRAINED by now, I dozed off, able to forget for a few minutes the itching of my eyes under the tape. Every so often, Rock would chuckle at some line in the movie, followed by a burst of short, strong sniffs of air. I would shift my position, resolve to pray, and then drowse for another few minutes.

The movie had just ended when I heard a different sound: a key in the door. I sat up straight with my hands under me, fingering the L-shaped slit in the vinyl seat of my chair where the stuffing was coming out. Steve came in on a trail of food odors, rustling bags, and jiggling ice.

I felt nauseated. Had he talked to Nan? What was she thinking now? What was she doing? *Stay calm, sweetheart.*

"Something to eat?" he said casually, walking over to stand near my chair.

"No. No, thanks."

"You better eat."

"I'm sorry. I couldn't eat anything now. Later, maybe." I couldn't imagine keeping anything in my stomach.

"You watch your health, don't you? You gotta take care of your health."

That's an odd remark, I wanted to tell him, a thread of anger tightening inside me, *considering your partner is ready to either shoot me or cut me into pieces if I so much as twitch the wrong way.* Instead, I said, "I'll drink some soda if you have it."

"Your wife," Steve began. "She ... "

I leaned forward. "Is she all right?" Anxiety must have thinned my voice.

"She's confused. I think she's not very bright," Steve said between mouthfuls.

"Remember, I told you. She's been traveling and just got back from a very long trip. She's exhausted. Besides, anyone would be confused by a call about a kidnapping."

"That's okay as long as she doesn't do anything stupid like call the police," Steve said. "I told her that. I told her to do as I say or you will be dead and her too."

How could I protect Nan and still prepare the kidnappers for any possible reaction? I tried again. "She was already under a lot of stress, and now she's probably terrified. She might call our daughter, Kathy, to help her out."

"All she has to do is listen. Is it so hard to listen?" Steve sounded more agitated.

35

Nan was so fragile under emotional stress lately that I shuddered to think of the terror and turmoil that Steve's phone call would have triggered. I knew she would call Kathy for support. Kathy—the steady, bright beacon in any family storm, even as a little girl. I hoped I could steer the kidnappers in her direction. *Be ready, good daughter.*

"My wife is one of the smartest people I know," I said evenly, "but too much stress can make her sick. Tell her you want to talk to Kathy." I hoped my voice sounded calm and reasonable. Surely they would see how cooperative I was.

"We will see," was Steve's curt answer.

In the sluggish afternoon, Steve and Rock took lengthy turns in the shower, letting me use the bathroom in between. They checked the TV periodically and seemed happy that there were no news reports about missing Silicon Valley executives. *Thank you, Nan.*

Steve left a second time for food, reminding me again about his tough, trigger-happy partner. By the time he returned a half hour later, with McDonald's bags this time, the NBA playoffs were just getting underway. I had watched last week and remembered the evening games started around 6:00. Dinnertime. Grateful for the distraction of the game and the absence of conversation, I ate.

When the game ended, Steve stood abruptly, clicked off the remote, and announced, "Time to go to the safe house."

I tensed, wondering what this new development meant. Hadn't they said *this*, this motel room, was a "safe house" when we arrived here this morning? Now another one? I sat passively, but alert while one of them—Steve, I think—made seemingly endless short trips from the room to the car. The room door opened and the car door closed in a regular rhythm for about fifteen minutes. What were they packing? I had no sense of the contents of the room since the blindfold had remained in place.

Then Steve said, "Okay. Ready to go."

"Want to chain him up?" Rock asked Steve for the second time that day.

36

As before, Steve seemed reluctant. "He's okay for now. He's cooperating," Steve answered. "But first time he does something stupid, we chain him." Rock came over to the chair and took my arm, pulling me upright.

"My eyes are really bothering me. They're burning bad. Can you take this tape off?" I was becoming bolder, but my discomfort was so extreme, I didn't care.

They didn't answer. Then, abruptly, a pair of hands yanked off my eye patches both at once. "Ahhh!" The sting was excruciating. Almost simultaneously, a second set of hands pulled into place a blindfold made of cloth. They made it tight, but it was far more comfortable than the duct tape. I could also better perceive light and dark through the fabric.

I was stiff from sitting on the hard vinyl seat for so many hours, and I stumbled as they guided me to the door. When I did so, I felt the gun barrel zero in against my ribs. They pushed me into the backseat again, but this time Steve drove and Rock was my guard.

We were on the freeway only briefly before we seemed to exit, angling to the right and slowing gradually before we came to a full stop. Then we turned onto a road where headlights penetrated my blindfold. They seemed close. Probably a two-lane highway.

"No lights behind us for a long time," said Steve.

"Good," grunted Rock. "A clean getaway, eh?" He made a barking sound that mingled with his sniffing. I supposed it was a laugh.

After twenty minutes or so, Steve slowed down considerably. We made several tight turns and came to a halt. He cut the engine. Rock got out first and pulled me behind him. In only a few steps, we were through a door and walking across a room.

"You're going to be a Boy Scout now," said Steve, almost jovially. His tone chilled me. "Ever been a Boy Scout?"

"I—ah … no, not really. Maybe for a while as a kid."

"Well, you're camping out here." He dropped something on the floor. "Your sleeping bag," he announced.

They guided me to the bathroom and then back to the pallet on the floor.

"I'll be sleeping right here in this room, so don't try anything," Steve warned tersely. "Now sleep."

Unbelievably, remarkably, I slept.

• • •

The Warnocks

THE SINGLE SHEET of note paper lay open on John Warnock's lap beneath the steering wheel as he stared rigidly ahead through the windshield. The clatter of shopping carts and a few laughing voices near his car in the Rancho Market parking lot dissolved into a fuzzy tunnel of sound. He knew he should act. Call the FBI. Do something, for God's sake! But it seemed he could barely lift the key to the ignition.

A seasoned executive, analytical thinker, creative problem-solver—and where did that get him now? Frozen with the fear that any action he took could end the life of his closest friend. John slammed the steering wheel with his palm in frustration.

The sting in his hand galvanized him. He shoved Nan's astonishing message into his pocket and headed home. He would talk to Marva. Together they would devise a plan to support Nan, find Chuck, and end this whole absurd episode.

"Good Lord, John, what's wrong?" Marva Warnock was instantly frightened by the look on her husband's face as he rushed into their house twenty minutes after his grocery store meeting with Nan. "Are you all right? Has someone died? What? *What?*"

"Read this," he said, unfolding the note on the kitchen counter before her.

Marva studied the note, and then looked at John. It was rare for John Warnock to be fearful or confused. In his eyes at this moment, his wife saw both. "You believe this, don't you?" she said with quiet anxiety.

John motioned Marva to a chair at the kitchen table. With the crumpled note in Nan's hurried, sloping script between them, John recounted for his wife the puzzling sequence of events at Adobe since 10:00 that morning, when Janice Coley had first asked him if he'd seen Chuck.

"It was the call from Kryzanowski that clinched it for me," he said. John Kryzanowski, longtime friend and personal financial manager for both the Warnocks and Geschkes, had called Adobe earlier that afternoon, concerned about the phone call he'd just received from Nan. When he couldn't reach Chuck, he asked for John Warnock.

"John said Nan sounded strange—really upset, distant," John told Marva. "When she wanted $650,000 in hundreds, he knew something was off. When I put that together with the rest of the events of the morning, I ... we—yeah, I believe it, Marv." He sank his head into his hands.

Marva was silent for a moment, struggling with emotion. Then she said with a calm, clear certainty, "We have to call the FBI right away."

"*No!*" John said, his shout landing on the tail of her words.

"Honey, if this is real, we have no choice," said Marva. Her voice was tight with tension.

"I want to, but we can't! Think of the risk, Marva!" He glared at her. "They could kill him. My God, they could *kill Chuck* if we call the police!"

Her voice wavered slightly. "You could be in danger, too."

John sighed. "I hear what you're saying, Marv, but you read the note same as I did. They told Nan explicitly, 'no police.' We cooperate and we get him back."

"John, listen. Without the police or FBI or anyone who has a ghost of an idea of how to deal with criminals, we'd be in way over our heads. And how could that possibly help Chuck?"

"On one level, I agree with you. But if we call, and something goes wrong, then we'd be responsible. If Chuck dies, could you live with that? Huh?" John rubbed his hand over his face in exasperation. Marva was both wrong and right. So was he. But a stalemate had to be more wrong than either of them.

For the next hour, John and Marva argued the issue of FBI involvement from every possible angle. The risks were enormous, whichever course they took. But when they'd worn the issue out, Marva hadn't wavered from her first instinct.

"Call them, John. Please," she said.

He reached for her hand and locked his eyes on hers. "Okay, Marv. I guess I always knew we'd have to do it. But I'm scared." His voice grew hoarse. "I've never been so scared."

"Me too," she whispered.

Somewhere finding a reserve of energy to override her fear, Marva turned to action. "I'll call Nan and tell her we want to call the FBI. The kids should be called, too. Nan's going to need them with her," she said.

"Her note says she's going to be at the college editing her video program. It's almost 6:00, so she's probably there," John said. "I'll find the Bureau number in the meantime." He left Marva dialing the kitchen phone while he went into the den.

. . .

Nan

IT WAS AFTER 5:00 when I showered and changed to go to the Foothills College TV studio. My editing session was scheduled for 6:00, and I hoped John would get there early so we could talk alone. I arrived at the college a little before 6:00 and tried to work before my crew arrived, but I was distracted and indecisive. My history project seemed irrelevant. When someone called me to the phone, I was relieved. I prayed it was John.

Even better, it was Marva. Over the years, Marva Warnock and I had become as close as our husbands, the four of us raising our children and building a business together. Marva was our practical side, our steady, no-nonsense voice, the one who grounded us firmly in reality.

"Look, Nan," she opened without preamble, "we've got to get the FBI involved. This is too big for us."

"I know, and I want to, but we just can't, Marva … I'm afraid they'll … they specifically said—"

"Yes, yes, I know," she shushed. "John didn't want to either at first, but we've been talking for the last hour and we're both convinced it's the only way. It's the right thing to do for Chuck, Nan. I think you know that."

Her obvious conviction reassured me. Though filled with fear at the thought of defying the kidnappers, I knew, at some deep level of my being, that Marva was right. I was at the end of my tether. My shell of control was slowly sloughing off, and soon I'd be down to raw skin. Maybe I had already harmed Chuck by my stupid mistakes.

I exhaled slowly, resigned to what I knew in my bones. "I guess you're right, Marva, I do need help. I'm just so scared … so scared …." My voice went raspy and I choked down the sobs I'd been holding since noon.

"Nan? Are you there? Are you okay?"

"I'm okay. Tell John to make the call, Marva." I made an effort to put resolve in my voice. With the words out, I had a guilty sense of relief.

"Good decision," she said briskly, masking her own emotion. "Stay put for the moment, and I'll call you right back with a plan."

I put the phone down with a quiet rush of affection and gratitude for Marva. A tight kernel of hope settled in my chest.

· · ·

The Warnocks

JOHN FOUND the local number for the FBI and jotted it on the telephone pad. Then he dropped into his old brown leather "thinking chair," as the kids called it, holding the thick Bay Area phone book in his lap. He heard the soothing hum of Marva's voice two rooms away.

Less than five minutes from now, he would be making a phone call that might change his life forever. He tried to close his eyes and build his resolve. He knew that calling the FBI was the right thing to do—the only thing to do. But whether his eyes were closed or open, he saw only Chuck's face.

"We'll get you out of this mess, buddy," he whispered. "We're all here for you: Nan and your kids, Marva and I, and our kids. Wherever you are, I hope you know that, Chuck." John smiled a little. "You're stuck with all of us for the rest of your life, pal." The weight of the final phrase struck his chest, and he stood abruptly. The phone book thudded to the floor.

John didn't know a man he respected more than Chuck Geschke. A man of strong ethics and high standards, with a brilliant mind and a biting wit. Yet Chuck was as comfortable to be around as an old shoe. "He just has this aura of kindness about him," Marva always said.

Gazing through the shutters to the bright green afternoon, John thought of their early days in the Xerox lab—how he and Chuck had made an instant professional and personal connection that had done nothing but grow stronger in the past fourteen years, how he and Chuck had worked those Xerox years side by side, sharing and containing the excitement as the significance of their work slowly became apparent.

Then the real test: leaving secure jobs at Xerox to build their own company exactly ten years ago, in '82. All they had then was intelligence, creativity, a talented team, and plenty of grit. But over and

42

through it all was their absolute faith in each other. *That was the key,* he thought.

He remembered renting the new offices in that first building on Marine Way in Mountain View. He could still see Chuck's dad, Matt, at eighty-one years old, lumbering in each day with his carpentry tools to build shelves for their overflowing collection of technical books.

There was the wild and crazy celebration in '83 when Steve Jobs signed the contract for Adobe to implement their Postscript software for the first Apple LaserWriter. It was still hard to believe, but that event launched Adobe Systems—and the whole world, as a matter of fact—into the era of desktop publishing.

That was their turning point. And they were only a year-old company! Adobe grew and prospered like an arrow shot from a quiver of jewels. From their early days in Mountain View, they had moved to Palo Alto and then back to Mountain View, to their present new, larger headquarters. In building Adobe, John felt like he and Chuck were architects as well as scientists. He loved what they were doing—not just with their products, but with their people. You could feel the buzz of excitement on every floor.

Every year Marva and Nan planned festive company events that brought employees together to celebrate the company's success. And Chuck was always in the middle of things. No high-handed executive distance for him. He could be a part of any group, regardless of their job status—just a regular guy in jeans, having his beer and talking sports or kids or anything you could name.

There was an *esprit* at Adobe that other companies envied. John swallowed with difficulty. What if—could it ever be the same without Chuck? He looked down at the number on the phone pad.

"John?" Marva had come in quietly behind him. It was still bright outside at 6:00 PM in May, but the room was shuttered and dim. She switched on the desk lamp. "I'm off the phone," she said.

"Is she okay with it?" he asked without turning around to face her.

"Yeah, she is. She said to go ahead." She gently turned John around by the shoulders to look at him. "She's scared to death, John, and she's close to breaking apart. But she knows she can't handle this alone any longer. She was actually grateful that we called."

The Warnocks held on to one another for a long moment. Then, taking the helm as he was accustomed to doing, the CEO of Adobe Systems stepped to the desk and reached for the phone.

· EVENING ·

FBI

K EN THOMPSON was shopping with his twelve-year-old daughter for his wife's birthday present when his pager buzzed about 6:30 Tuesday evening. His daughter made a face. She'd been in a law-enforcement family long enough to know what the sound meant. Thompson, supervisory special agent (SSA) for the San Jose office of the FBI, hurried his disappointed daughter back home and called his office.

"We've got a possible major seven in Los Altos," his duty agent, Russ Atkinson, told him. The original call would have been routed to the complaint line in San Francisco for screening. The bounce-back call to Thompson's office meant there could be legs on this one. He listened intently. A "seven" was a kidnapping: extremely rare and always dangerous.

The information was sketchy. "SF says the guy that called was suspicious as hell—paranoid," said Russ. "Wouldn't give the name of the victim, wouldn't say what time it happened. Nada. Wants to talk to us in person. See our badges."

Despite all that, SF thought the caller was credible—and scared. Thompson noted the name and address in Los Altos, told his family not to expect him home until they saw him, and headed to his office to mobilize a team.

His first call went back to San Francisco to his boss Dick Held, the special agent in charge (SAC) and senior command of the San Francisco office of the FBI. With SAC Held notified and accessible, he called Atkinson back and dispatched him to the Warnock home in Los Altos to conduct the initial interview with John Warnock.

Next SSA Thompson called in Larry Taylor, a veteran agent of the Bureau's violent crime unit in San Francisco and one of few with direct experience in the rare crime of kidnapping. Special Agent (SA) Taylor, currently assigned to the Hayward office, had been case agent on the Michaela Garrett abduction in 1988, had been part of the Patty Hearst team in the '70s, and was a highly skilled interrogator. Thompson wanted Taylor to question the wife.

By 8:00 PM, Agent Thompson had Agent Taylor on the road to Los Altos, specialized agents standing by in San Jose, and an emergency office center organized for information relay. If the call proved to be the real thing, the Bureau was ready.

About 8:30, Marva Warnock opened her door to a thickset, muscular man in his late forties with a boyish face and disarmingly gentle manner. He pulled out a badge. "FBI, ma'am. Special Agent Larry Taylor, senior resident agent, Hayward, California." Taylor was so thorough and courteous that Marva opened the door without further question and ushered him into the living room where Agent Atkinson had just returned from Foothills College with Nan.

• • •

Nan

A LITTLE BEFORE 8:00, an FBI agent named Russ Atkinson arrived at the Foothills studio to pick me up. I excused myself from the edit session, telling my colleagues that a former classmate had just come to town and tracked me down. Whether they bought the explanation or not, we were all glad for a reason to end our strained meeting. At least I felt they were glad to see *me* go.

The agent drove me back to the Warnock's house, and from the moment the door opened, I was encircled not only by John and Marva's arms, but by their genuine care and concern. Marva led me to a comfortable chair and, in minutes, had a sandwich before me and a glass of wine in my hand.

I had not sat down to rest since the kidnapper's phone call, nearly eight hours ago. Nor had I eaten since breakfast. My body sagged against the soft cushions. In that moment of release, I realized that my jaw had been clenched and my shoulders hunched in tension for hours.

The respite didn't last. Another agent arrived at the Warnocks on my heels, asking to talk with me. They gave me about ten minutes to rest before Larry Taylor, a kindly looking man, settled me in the study to begin questioning.

Agent Atkinson went back to Adobe with John to search Chuck's office and round up inadvertent witnesses. At their request, but with some misgiving, I handed the agents my house keys, my car keys, and the keys to Chuck's office. The FBI was officially involved.

After a half hour in the study, I didn't think Agent Larry Taylor was so kind. It was clear by then that I was under suspicion. This wasn't "questioning"; this was interrogation.

"You and your husband getting along okay, Mrs. Geschke?" he asked.

"What do you mean?"

"You know, arguments, suspicions—that sort of thing?"

"Suspicious of *each other*? Absolutely not! And we argue about the same as any married couple. Nothing unusual." I gritted my teeth. This line of questioning was getting us nowhere.

"Long business trips? Women?"

"What are you suggesting?"

"How about your sons? Either of them having problems with their dad?"

For the next three hours, Taylor focused his lens on our marriage, our family life, and our close friends. Did we have any ongoing disputes? Would Chuck have reason to disappear? I continually pulled him back to the phone call from the kidnappers and the urgency of what I needed to do.

I tried desperately to make Agent Taylor understand how important it was to comply with the kidnappers. They were criminals! And dangerous! He ignored me and returned to the marriage issue, inferring—now not so subtly—that I may have set up this elaborate scheme to end my marriage and grab the money.

It was after 11:00 PM when I first felt that Larry Taylor had eliminated me and the children as suspects and was ready to delve into other scenarios. But I was too weary and frazzled to appreciate the change of direction.

"Take a little break," he said softly and left the room.

I barely had time to use the bathroom and had just begun to splash my face with cool water when Marva knocked. "They're ready for you, honey," she said.

"Ready for what?" I asked her, opening the door.

An unfamiliar agent stepped in front of Marva. "We have a few more questions for you, ma'am," he said. Then as an afterthought, "If you don't mind, ma'am."

Of course I mind, you idiot! My husband is missing, in the hands of violent criminals, and we're all sitting in this comfortable house asking stupid questions. You're supposed to be helping me get him back. That's the only reason I agreed to call you. No one understands! I have to do what they say. I have to get the money to them. You're not helping me!

Feeling helpless, I followed the agent back into the study and took

48

my seat. We spent about an hour going over Chuck's work life: his coworkers, his clients, how he spent his days, who he traveled with, who might have reason to hate him or resent him.

Finally, I stood up and said, "This is enough. Is any of this information going to help to get my husband back?"

The agent stood, too, and had the grace to be conciliatory. "Sorry, ma'am. It's procedure. And yes, ma'am, we need to know as much as we can to make good decisions. Believe me, getting Mr. Geschke back is our only goal here. But we need to get you home now. We'll talk again tomorrow."

Tomorrow was already today. I had been exhausted when the day began, and now I was shaky and a little dizzy with fatigue and the effects of continuous adrenalin surges. I needed to sleep, but not in our house all alone. I longed to call the children, but the FBI said no, not yet.

"I'm not going home," I announced suddenly as we returned to the living room with the others. "I intend to stay here at the Warnocks tonight."

"Not a good idea," said Agent Taylor, who seemed to be in charge of this crew.

"You need to be at home in case the phone rings, Nan," John said quietly.

I saw the wisdom of that. I nodded, and added, "And in case anyone is watching the house, we want things to look normal. They have to think I'm doing what they want."

"Yes. That's right," Taylor said. He began gathering his tapes and equipment.

I hugged Marva and John once more and got in Agent Taylor's car to ride the few blocks to our house on University. Neither of us spoke. Despite his presence, all I could think of was my utter aloneness. My beloved Chuck was in terrible danger. My children had no idea what was happening. I had just left my best friends standing on their doorstep. Even the prospect of being in our family home didn't comfort me. I was deeply, profoundly afraid.

My eyes were slipping shut when we stopped in front of the house. When the car stopped and the motor died, I lifted my head. Instantly, my eyes snapped wide open and I sat up straight. The house was ablaze with light. Several cars were lined up across the front and in the driveway. The doors were open, and at least four men in black jackets buzzed back and forth, trailing wires from point to point, talking into bulky portable phones and testing the alarms.

"What is going on?" I cried out. I raced from the car to the house. "Who are you? What are you doing in my house?" I shouted, horrified at the scene before me and the implications I could only imagine.

"Crawling with police" were the words bouncing from wall to wall in my head. If the kidnappers saw this, they'd know for sure I had called the police. Oh, God! What would they do to Chuck now? It was all my fault for giving in.

"Your badges! Let me see your badges! *Now!*" I was shrieking by this time. I saw them look at one another and then at Larry Taylor. They pulled out their ID cards. FBI, all of them. Not that I was surprised. Then a woman walked by the open door inside the house. Another agent inside. *Crawling with police ...*

Gradually, Taylor herded all of us inside, closed the door, and managed to get most of the outside and some of the inside lights turned off. I was breathing through my clenched teeth, trying to contain my anger and frustration.

"Look, Mrs. Geschke—Nan—we have to do this work in your house so we can catch these guys and get your husband free. Phones have to be tapped, the security system has to be wired to ours, we have to search Chuck's personal items, and so on. It's all part of the investigation. It's our job."

I felt defeated. Everything was out of my hands, it seemed. "I guess so. Okay. But please move your cars to the back and keep the lights down." I was still shaken and uncertain. "I'd like to call Mrs. Warnock to come and spend the night here with me," I told Agent Taylor.

"I think that's a good idea," he said.

I picked up the phone in the kitchen. Nothing. No dial tone! "This phone is dead!" I shouted. "What's going on? The kidnapper could be trying to call this minute!" Once more my fear and anger mounted and broke in giant waves.

"Please stay calm, ma'am," one of the agents said. "Maybe they're working on that line outside. Here, use my portable."

I grabbed his phone and punched in the Warnocks' number. No ring. Nothing. The mobile phone was dead, too. And *this* was the FBI? I snapped.

"*Out!* Get out of my house. All of you. *Out! Out!* I don't know who you are or what you're doing here. You've botched up everything. *Leave. Now.*"

I screamed and pushed them, sounding, I'm sure, as hysterical as I felt. One of them tried to hold my arms down and shove me backward, but his companion quickly pulled him away.

A calm, authoritative voice—Taylor's—overrode the commotion: "Outside, everyone." They left me shaking with my head in my hands. I locked the door behind them and then rushed through the house, locking every door and checking every window, pulling shades and closing shutters. I had to protect myself. Who were these people? They had rewired my security system and cut off my phones. I could reach no one to help me.

They could be the kidnappers. They could be posing as the FBI. What are they going to do to me? Are they going to find the children, too? Dear God, I don't know what to do. Only you can help me now.

Utterly alone, I curled into a chair in the dark bedroom—our bedroom, Chuck's and mine. It was 3:00 AM. *Chuck, I love you.*

I had begun to doze off when the doorbell chimed—once, twice, then again. I sat up straight, heart racing. I checked the clock: 3:30 AM. The doorbell again ... then firm staccato knocking. I ran to the front hall and peered cautiously through the small window flanking the door. John and Marva were on the front steps with the agents still milling in the yard behind them.

I think John sensed my presence. "Nan," he said urgently, pressing close to the seam of the door. "It's Marva and John. Please let us in. We need to talk."

I hesitated barely ten seconds before unlocking the door. John and Marva were the only people I knew I could trust right now, and I wanted them close to me. "But not them," I said firmly when two of the agents began to follow them inside. "They're totally incompetent. They cut off the phones and ... and how do I know they're really the FBI?"

John took me by the shoulders and locked his eyes on mine. "Nan, listen to me," he said levelly. "These men are legitimate FBI agents. I promise you. They called us to come and talk to you. We need them badly if we're going to be able to help Chuck." One by one, the agents gradually slipped inside the house behind John and fanned through the house.

"You can't do this alone, Nan," Marva said. "We need these men, and we need each other."

I looked from one to the other. I saw their love for Chuck and me and also their fear for us all. "I know I need help. I just don't know who I can trust, besides you. I'm suspicious of everyone. All I know is if I make a mistake—'*Don't do anything stupid or we'll cut him up in pieces and put him on your doorstep—*' if I do something stupid, they'll hurt him, they'll kill him ... " I put my head in my hands and began to cry softly. " ... because of me."

Marva put her arm around me and led me to the family room. "Well, that won't happen because you're doing everything right. Now, while the agents finish up with the phones and the house, we're going to call the children. Never mind what the FBI told you. You need them, too, Nan."

"And they deserve to know what's going on," added John.

"But first," Marva said, "we're calling your doctor. Anyone under this kind of stress needs help to cope. And you *have* to sleep or you'll collapse."

Marva picked up the phone—it was working by now—and John left to talk with the agents upstairs. I lay my head back against the chair and closed my eyes, resting on the solid wall of John and Marva's strength.

WEDNESDAY | MAY 27

· MORNING ·

Kathy

KATHY GESCHKE spent most of Tuesday alone in her San Francisco Bayside Village apartment, happily making plans. She updated her job prospect list, confirmed an interior design interview for later in the week, and chatted with her mother twice about dates and flights for the family vacation on Nantucket at the end of June. They had tried, but still couldn't find a good date for Nan to come to the city for a fitting for her mother-of-the-groom dress.

By late morning, still in her pj's, Kathy was focused on her computer screen, absorbed in designing a bridal shower invitation for her sister-in-law-to-be, Diane. The shower was only a few weeks off, and Kathy wanted the invitations in the mail—soon!

The afternoon evaporated, and the day slid into dusk. Satisfied with the invitations, Kathy switched on the desk lamp and began to review her interior design portfolio for the upcoming interview. Engrossed in her editing, she skipped dinner and worked late into the evening. On one quick trip to the kitchen for a diet soda and a handful of pretzels, she caught her reflection in the hallway mirror and laughed. "Holy disaster," she said. Her bright blond, chin-length hair was flattened into grooves where she'd run her fingers through it, and her usually alert blue eyes were drooping and pale with strain. Still, she pushed on until she had reviewed every sample in the portfolio, replacing several with newer work. When she finally fell into bed, satisfied at last with her efforts, it was already Wednesday morning.

Tired as she was, sleep wasn't immediate. She was still riding the wave of energy and optimism generated by the excitement of the previous weekend. Graduation. The party her parents gave to celebrate her achievement. She was a college graduate!

It hadn't been a straight path. Community college first, then the transfer to USF, then the growing certainty that she was an artist. Though her agenda was always filled with art projects, Kathy clearly remembered the career test that had cleared her vision for the future. She'd scored off the charts in interior design. Not really surprising for a little girl who, for years, had rearranged her bedroom every couple of months.

She smiled into the darkness. That saucy little girl now had her fine arts degree and new credibility in the design work she loved. The future was wide open, she decided, and she would make her mark. Brimming with contentment, she drifted into sleep.

When the phone rang about 4:15 AM, Kathy resisted the sound and struggled backward into her dream. It had been a good one, and she didn't want to lose it. But the fragments slowly dissolved into a gray mist. Eyes still closed, she groped for the phone.

"Yes? Hello?" she said in a sleep-thick voice.

"Kathy, it's Mom."

An alarm bell buzzed in her brain. She sat upright, fully alert. Her mother's voice was flat and stiff, as though tightly stretched over a dangerous void. "Mom? What's wrong? Is something wrong?"

Kathy, like her brothers, was alert to her mother's emotional highs and lows. For many years, Nan had been susceptible to anxiety attacks, triggered mostly by stress and an inability to sleep. The siblings knew how to help. When anxiety threatened, they circled the family wagons around her, learned how to isolate the stress triggers, and wrapped her with love until equilibrium returned—usually very soon.

Things had worsened for a time after her mother's sister Kathy—Kathy Geschke's namesake—was killed seven years ago, but she'd had no bad spells in a long time, until the flare-up on the Russia return flight. Kathy's heart lurched. Was Mom faced with some new stress?

"It's about your Dad. Daddy." Her mother's voice was still unnatural, shaking now. "He's been kidnapped, Kathy. Kidnapped and held for ransom."

In fear and confusion, Kathy shouted into the phone: "*What? What are you saying, Mom? For God's sake, we just had dinner together a day ago. This is bizarre.*"

Nan plowed on, her voice rising and thinning like a narrow ribbon fraying on both sides. "And they're watching us. I know they're watching. They're going to kill him, cut him up, and feed him to the sharks!!" The word "sharks" was sliced by a sob.

Then another voice broke in, low-pitched, controlled, and firm, though she caught an overlay of anxiety. "Kathy, it's John Warnock."

"John? You're at our house?" Her heart rate accelerated. "Is this some kind of sick joke? What's wrong with Mom? Someone better tell me what the hell is going on!" Belligerence suited her better, helped to control her rising fear.

"Stay calm, Kathy. What your mother told you is true. Your dad was abducted from our parking lot at Adobe sometime this morning. We need you to come home, Kathy."

This morning. She remembered her mother's concern that Chuck hadn't been seen in the office, that he hadn't called her back as he promised. How dismissive she had been in reassuring her mother. Her conversation had been almost flippant—her only thought to save herself and her mother from worry. *Oh, Dad! Maybe I could have helped … I'm so sorry, Dad.* She began to cry quietly.

"I'm on my way, John," she said, struggling to keep the tears at bay. With effort, she made her words brisk and decisive.

"Wait, honey," he said. "We're sending someone for you. An FBI agent. The FBI wants to pick you up."

She breathed in sharply. "No! It'll take too long. I'm not waiting!" The last thing she wanted was someone controlling what she could or couldn't do. She wouldn't allow it. Then, another thought intruded: "Am I in danger?"

"Possibly," John answered. "We don't know much yet, Kathy. We've had only one phone call from the kidnappers, but they told your mother repeatedly that they were watching her and the house."

"I can't believe what I'm hearing. How's Mom doing with this?"

"Strong, so far. Tough. Scared, like we all are. But she's totally exhausted—hasn't slept or eaten for hours, and the agents have been questioning her nonstop. She's got to be close to the edge. She needs you, Kathy. We'll have an agent at your apartment in less than an hour."

"Okay," she whispered, "I'll be waiting." She suddenly felt more like a small girl than a twenty-four-year-old college graduate.

Kathy replaced the phone on the base and saw that her hand was shaking. Her feet seemed heavy, and her gait was slow and clumsy as she walked to the bedroom. "Stay focused," she told herself. "Take a shower, brush your teeth, and find some clothes."

She repeated instructions to herself like a mantra as she found a duffel bag and filled it with jeans, underwear, shoes, and makeup. She let the voice fill her head, leaving no room for the deluge of thoughts pushing against her brain, pounding in her temples. She wouldn't let them in—not yet.

When the front door buzzer sounded, Kathy was ready. Sluggishly, she picked up her purse, hoisted her bag on her shoulder, and opened the door to a tall, sandy-haired man who showed her his badge and identified himself as an FBI agent. The reality of an officer of the law standing on her doorstep suddenly struck her and made her legs weak.

As the agent turned to lead her toward his car, Kathy froze behind him. She felt a crack in the thick screen of protection she had built inside herself. Pain and fear rushed in and energized her.

"I'll drive myself," she told the agent abruptly. "I have to be alone right now." She was vaguely aware of her audacity in giving instructions to an officer, but it didn't deter her. "Just follow me. Please." The final word was a belated courtesy, not a request. Kathy turned toward her designated parking space, leaving the agent no time for discussion. She saw his lips press into a tight line, but he got in his car and fell in behind her.

As soon as she was moving along the interstate in her silver Honda Civic, Kathy felt better. She had taken some control back. Anger and powerful love welled up and mixed together, fueling her resolve to help her mom and rescue her dad. Whatever it took. There would be a way, and she would find it.

Kathy Geschke never was a sideliner. Indecision irritated her. Her friends had quickly learned that with Kathy, no precious time would ever be wasted deciding what assignment to tackle, what restaurant to choose, or what movie to see. Quick, practical action could solve just about anything, she believed. *Hold on, Dad, I'm on my way.*

She set the cruise control and checked her rearview mirror. The agent was close behind. Annoying as it usually was to be "watched over," Kathy was glad for his presence. It was dark, not yet 6:00 AM. Traffic was sparse, and the winking red taillights in the distance seemed to warn of danger ahead. She concentrated on action. What should she do first when she got home? Check on Mom. Talk to Pete.

The smooth, even speed of the car calmed her, and all at once Kathy could think only of her dad's tribute to her at the graduation party, his favorite, proud-father way of showing his love and delight in his only daughter. She smiled into the faintly rising light of morning.

"If I'm ever marooned on a desert island," he had said to the party guests and would often say to her brothers—or anyone who would listen for the tenth time!—"I hope Kathy is the one with me. Not you guys"—he always exaggerated the tease to Peter and John—"you guys would be looking for a pizza carryout or whining that you didn't have cable TV. But Kathy? Kathy'd be cutting down banana trees and building a goldarned *boat!*"

Just as fresh tears began to blur her vision, she reached the exit ramp for El Camino Road. She slowed and curved off, the Bureau's black sedan in her shadow. Almost home. At this moment, Kathy wanted nothing more than to wrap her arms around her mother and stand beside the solid presence of her older brother.

◆ ◆ ◆

Peter

TWENTY-SIX-YEAR-OLD Peter Geschke paced the kitchen, stopping at intervals to stare out the window over the sink that faced the street. It was approaching 7:30 AM, and the day had brightened a good deal since he'd arrived at the family home about an hour ago.

According to John Warnock, Kathy should be here any moment. Peter rolled his shoulders—five times forward, five times back. Then he fingered the tight cords in his neck. Fear for his sister's safety pressed in on him. His mother's safety, too. When he knew Nan and Kathy were in the same house, he'd feel a little more secure. *If we can ever feel secure again.*

He wanted his brother John there, too, though with John across the country at school in New Jersey, that was out of the question. All of them together would be a block of strength, a formidable wall of family that no criminal could scale. Together they would find a way to bring Chuck back to them. He was sure of it. *I'll keep them safe until you're back, Dad.*

His siblings would no doubt roll their eyes at his rescue images. Peter half-smiled. They had teased him for years about being the dreamer, the idealist in the family. Dad teased him, too, but Peter had always been secure in his father's pride. He swallowed over the lump rising in his throat, remembering with gratitude how they all valued and relied on his fierce, big-brother loyalty, his compassion, his identity as a "different drummer." "My family!" he whispered into the stillness of the kitchen. He longed to talk with Diane.

"You okay, son?" John Warnock entered the kitchen quietly. He joined Peter at the window and gave him a sympathetic pat on the shoulder.

"Better than an hour ago—physically speaking," Peter answered.

John chuckled without much mirth. "Had a devil of a time waking you up."

"I know. Sorry about that. I still feel a little sick, but at least I'm coherent now."

When John had called him about 4:30 AM, Peter was in a profoundly deep sleep. He hadn't felt well for days and had stayed home from work the previous Thursday and Friday. He was still under the weather on Monday, and he and Diane left early from the Memorial Day graduation party for Kathy.

After arriving home in Fremont, a thirty-minute drive from Los Altos, Diane picked up her car and left for her apartment, while Peter went straight to bed, well dosed with a nighttime cold medicine. He went to work Tuesday, but still sick, took more cold medicine and went to sleep early again that night. The phone must have rung a dozen times before it penetrated his consciousness. Nor could John's voice on the answering machine break into his lingering grogginess.

"Wake up, Pete! Pick up the phone," John said over and over, with growing irritation.

"Huh? Who? John? John Warnock?" Peter ground the receiver against his ear.

"Yes, Pete. It's John. Wake up, son. Your father's been kidnapped. We need you at home. And please, don't call Diane—not yet."

Peter stared at the receiver in confusion and disbelief. When he awakened enough to absorb the message, his mind fought an odd battle between sluggishness and the hyperspeed of panic. A middle school math teacher, his first clear thought was to get his lesson plans to school for the substitute teacher they'd have to call for him.

"Peter! Are you there? Pete!"

"I'll be there as soon as I can, John," he said thickly. "I have to get a plan to school. I need to stop there first."

Peter slogged from room to room of the small house that he and his new bride would share in just a couple of months. Something was out of place, some alarm bell was beating in his brain, but he couldn't find its source. Willing himself to focus, he found his textbooks and briefcase, and hastily constructed plans for Wednesday's classes. Then he showered, shaved, and dressed. He pulled into the school parking lot before 6:00 AM.

Peter's lethargy had disappeared by 6:30, the time he reached the house on University Avenue, but the dull headache, sore throat—and the sense of alarm—persisted. Peter rubbed his eyes and ran a hand through his straight coppery hair.

Built like Chuck, Peter was tall and strong, but of all the siblings, seemed most like his mother in looks and manner. Perhaps he understood her best, too. Their generous, sensitive natures were alike. Peter was worried about the stress bearing down on his mother—on all of them—and mentally urged Kathy to drive faster. Her presence would help.

John left Peter at the window while he crossed the kitchen to pour them some coffee. John took a seat at the kitchen table, and Peter continued to pace, circling the warm mug with both hands, until they heard the garage door groan to life. Kathy's Honda had pulled in.

• • •

Kathy

"KATH," WAS ALL Peter said when she opened the door into the back hall situated between Chuck's study and the living room. He reached for her, and she let herself fall against him. Kathy was tall and solidly built, but her brother's large-framed height easily enveloped her. John and Marva Warnock circled their arms around them both.

Pulling back, Kathy scanned the living room. A couple of people in dark clothes were talking in low voices at the far end. At least four others hustled importantly in and out of the house, checking phone lines and obviously monitoring the street and yard from all sides. FBI agents, she assumed, as the agent who escorted her to the house walked over to join the little group in the living room. "Where's Mom?" she asked.

"Upstairs," Marva answered. "Sleeping, we hope. How anyone could handle a day like yesterday is hard to imagine. The pressure on her is incredible."

"She was on the ragged edge by around 3:00 AM, just before we called you and Pete," John said.

"I finally got her doctor on the phone and filled him in," said Marva. "He suggested some medication for her and said he'd stop by later this morning."

"Mostly, she needs sleep," said Peter.

Still talking quietly, Kathy moved with the others across the living room, up the few steps to the dining room and from there into the kitchen and adjacent den. Marva poured coffee and tried to coax everyone to eat.

"Maybe later, Marva. I'd throw up if I had a bite of anything right now," said Kathy. "I've been queasy since Mom's call this morning."

"Same with me," Pete said. "Thanks, but just coffee right now."

Marva nodded and sat down with the others in the den while John gave Kathy and Pete a full chronology of events since he and Janice Coley had searched the Adobe campus for Chuck the morning before. Soon after, John left to get ready for the work day at Adobe, and Marva followed him home to get some sleep until she was needed again.

Kathy and Peter went over John Warnock's account a second time, trying to find a crack, a reason, a solution for the bizarre event that had overtaken every thought and emotion in their minds.

"The FBI keeps asking me about our friends," Pete told her. "They want to know about everyone at your graduation party."

"Just a few close friends," Kathy said slowly, thinking. "The only person we didn't know real well was the guy who used to play football for Stanford. I forget who he came with, but I had met him at least once before."

"I talked with him for a while," Pete said, "but I couldn't even *invent* a good reason why he or anyone we know would want to harm Dad."

They focused on the money angle, straining to think who might have engineered such a plan—and why.

"Nothing makes sense!" Pete said. "What in the hell is happening here? The FBI is scrambling for a theory as much as we are. Bottom line, nobody knows anything." He stood up abruptly, poured more coffee, and resumed his pacing in the kitchen.

Her brother's frustration and simmering anger echoed in Kathy's ears like the hollow thump of an amplified heartbeat. She could almost taste the grains of fear like sand in her mouth. The police had no information, no clues. The FBI was their best hope, but they didn't even have a theory. Kathy didn't like relying on strangers, trained professionals or not. It was *her* Dad, not theirs. *Oh, Dad! Please be okay.*

"I hate feeling helpless," she hissed through tight lips. "We have to figure out a way to *do* something—now," she said. "You can't just take somebody's freedom away and control his family. You can't!" She hit her fist on the sofa cushion and let the tears come.

Pete turned toward her, his eyes filled with pain. He knelt beside her chair. "Want to pray, Kath?"

She took a long, deep, wobbly breath and pushed her hair behind her ears. "Yeah, I guess." She put her head in her hands as Pete began the first decade of the Rosary, the soothing repetitive prayer they'd both learned as children.

"*Hail Mary, full of grace ...* " they intoned in soft voices.

" *... the Lord is with you,*" said a third voice.

Kathy lifted her head and then sprang up to reach for Nan who had come into the den and joined in the prayer. "Mom! Oh, Mom!"

" *... now and at the hour of our death,*" Peter's baritone concluded the prayer, and the words trailed over them like the fine threads of a net as the three clung together.

♦ ♦ ♦

FBI

SPECIAL AGENT LARRY TAYLOR checked on the family in the kitchen. Mrs. Geschke had slept some, had a doctor on call, and seemed a little calmer. What a night she had—they all had. Though she still looked pale and shaken, she was making toast, replenishing the coffee, and coaxing her two grown children to eat. Taylor was glad she had something to occupy her, even briefly. Every minute without progress made them all more anxious, agents and family alike.

A glance at his watch told him it was time to leave for his meeting with the newly assigned agent-in-charge. He was more than ready to hand over responsibility for the family and the Los Altos site to the behavioral profiling unit. His work would be in the San Jose office from now on, preparing for a money drop, an arrest, and hopefully, a rescue.

Taylor quietly signed out with the agents on duty and walked to a coffee shop on Main Street in the village of Los Altos, a few blocks from the Geschke house on University, where Special Agent Dr. Mary Ellen O'Toole was waiting for him as arranged. Tired and drained from his emotional all-night duty call, the sight of Agent O'Toole revived him. Mary Ellen was young, soft-spoken, poised, and pretty, all of which belied her formidable expertise in criminal and victim behaviors. As the profile coordinator for the San Francisco field office, Mary Ellen was a key resource in advising Bureau agents as well as local police on the best tactics for crime resolution.

Taylor often thought that this smallish woman with curling, red-blond hair and gentle eyes was probably the direct opposite of what the TV-saturated public envisioned as an FBI agent. Though only in her thirties, SA O'Toole was no novice. She had eleven years with the Bureau, highly specialized behavioral training, hostage negotiation training, direct experience with the most dangerous criminals, and the genuine respect of her colleagues—Larry Taylor among them.

At a small table toward the back of the shop, Agent Taylor told Agent O'Toole every detail of the case, from the moment John Warnock made the initial call through the interrogation of Nan, Nan's fear and fury and suspicion, her midnight lockout of the FBI, her residual mistrust of the agents stationed in the house, the reported dialogue of the kidnapper's phone call, and the recent arrivals of Peter and Kathy Geschke. Mary Ellen listened intently, asked questions, took notes, and occasionally sipped her cooling coffee. Over an hour later, she stood and smiled at him.

"Thanks for the briefing, Larry," she said. "I need to get back to prep them for the next phone call. It could come any time."

Larry swallowed the rest of his coffee and picked up the check. "Remember, I'm your support in the San Jose office. You need anything, just give me the word and you'll have it."

With Mary Ellen in place to manage the family and the kidnapper communications, Larry would snatch a few hours of sleep and then report to the San Jose office to help set strategy for the ground operation when the time came. They needed to determine a location—soon. The more time that elapsed between abduction and contact, the colder the trail and the less chance for recovery. Larry prayed the family wouldn't realize that as the day dragged on.

"One more thing." Larry stopped speaking as they approached the cash register to pay. When they were alone again on the sidewalk, he said, "The wife had an overload of stress yesterday. Might be better to have someone else handle the rest of the calls—the son or daughter, maybe."

"Yes. I'll size things up and get some input from the other agents. We'll have to make a quick decision and do some scripting," Mary Ellen said.

"What I hear from the brother and the friends, the daughter is a take-charge kid," Larry added. "She might be your girl."

They walked back saying little, weighed down by the drama and danger that experience told them lay dead ahead.

· AFTERNOON ·

Kathy

J UST BEFORE NOON, a new agent came in through the back door
with Agent Taylor. Kathy felt an instant shift in the atmosphere
of the room. Was it relief? Energy? Purpose? Or threat? Whatever it
was, the attractive newcomer had caused it. Kathy struggled to read
the young redheaded woman who had clearly taken charge.

Agent Taylor introduced her and the woman turned toward them,
offering her hand to Nan, Peter, and Kathy in turn. "I'm Mary Ellen
O'Toole," she said, repeating her name with a nice, if practiced, smile.
Friendly, but reserved, Kathy decided. Professional.

"I'm a behavioral analyst for the Bureau. Also called a criminal
profiler. I'll be your main contact at the house from now on," Agent
O'Toole told them. "And please, call me Mary Ellen."

Peter said, "So you're gonna try to predict what these jerks will do
with Dad? Is that it?"

"You could say that," replied Mary Ellen, "but it's so we can prevent
them from doing anything." She appeared unfazed by Pete's barely
concealed skepticism.

"I'll also be trying to learn everything I can about your dad," she went on. "How he dresses, how he thinks, how he manages his employees, how he organizes his desk, his closet—anything that will give us clues about how he's likely to react in this situation. The information helps us negotiate with the kidnappers and ultimately protect your dad, which is our primary job." Mary Ellen O'Toole projected a certainty that was calming.

Speaking to the three of them, but looking directly at Kathy, Mary Ellen said, "As soon as everyone is ready, we'll sit down and begin to set our strategy."

Kathy felt a swell of hope. Here was a woman who would take action. Though Mary Ellen O'Toole could hardly be more than a dozen years older than she, Kathy was encouraged by the confidence and professionalism she conveyed.

"I'm ready now." Kathy tried to smile, but her lips were tight. Even so, she felt stronger. The assurance of a family meeting with a specific plan to follow gave her relief and hope.

Mary Ellen left them to walk Larry Taylor to the door and meet with the other agents on site. Kathy, Nan, and Peter filed silently into the living room.

• • •

FBI

SPECIAL AGENT O'TOOLE sat in an armless straight chair facing the three people hunched together on the sofa before her. Nan Geschke kept her head down, absently twisting the wedding ring on her left hand. Her posture was defeated, her face haunted. Peter followed every movement in the room, jittery, ready to challenge anyone or anything. Mary Ellen knew he was afraid, but understood his edge of belligerence. A man who felt powerless. How many times had she seen that look in the face of a victim? Kathy looked frightened, too, but with a frowning energy behind it, as if she were coiled to spring. *Yes, she might be the one to take the calls,* Mary Ellen thought.

As she watched them quietly trying to shore up one another with a protective arm or an understanding word, Mary Ellen felt a familiar anger stirring—anger at criminals who put good people through unspeakable fear and anguish. As she often did, Mary Ellen seethed inside at the injustice of it. But she had learned to quickly swallow her outrage, step back into her professional self, and turn to the business at hand.

"We don't have much time," she said briskly. "The kidnapper's going to call back today, and it's likely to be around the same time as yesterday. That means within the next hour or two. I'm going to need your help to stay ahead of the clock."

All three Geschkes nodded. "Just tell us what to do," said Nan.

"First, you'll tell me about Chuck," Mary Ellen said. "Everything you can think of about his personality, his disposition, his habits. Show me his desk, his closet, his drawers. Try to find any notes he's written, the books and newspapers he reads." She glanced at her watch: nearly 1:00 PM.

Mary Ellen continued, "I'll take notes and ask questions as we go. When I have an overview, we'll stop and script the phone call."

"How can you write a script if you don't know what he's going to say?" Kathy asked, crossing her arms, testing.

"We know he needs to give you instructions in order to get the money. And we know the basic kidnapper profile. Based on that, I'll give you some options to bring up during the call. There are ways for us to influence him without his knowing it. For instance, we want to keep him calm and confident that his plan is working. Right now, that's the best way to protect your dad."

"Oh. But what if … " Kathy was frowning in concentration.

Mary Ellen needed to redirect them. All three Geschkes looked tense and confused. Time was too short to give them the explanations they deserved.

"Take a minute to get your thoughts together while I check on the phones. Try to relax."

Mary Ellen walked the length of the living room to the bay window overlooking the backyard. She watched two agents in black jackets working diligently on some wiring at the back of the house. Probably testing the tracers they'd just installed on the phones. One of them was continually checking his watch. Fortunately, they were all accustomed to working under pressure. In the Bureau, their days were defined by it, and, like today, lives were usually hanging in the balance as they worked.

It was past time to decide who would handle the call. Mary Ellen reviewed the options. In their brief meeting after she arrived, she and her fellow agents had considered substituting Mary Ellen or another female agent for Nan Geschke. Too risky. The kidnapper knew Nan's voice ... but not Kathy's. Could Mary Ellen convince the kidnapper that Nan was ill and that *she* was Kathy? Maybe worth a try but still risky. The kidnapper obviously knew a great deal about the Geschke family. He might ask questions Mary Ellen couldn't answer, tipping him off to a police presence.

Her colleagues' opinion of Kathy's character and stamina throughout the morning was positive. Though she was young, they believed she had will and strength. Even in the short time she'd observed the family, Mary Ellen agreed. They would go with Kathy. She hastily returned to the anxious family still sitting rigidly side by side on the sofa, talking in low voices, waiting.

"Mrs. Geschke, I've been thinking," Mary Ellen began, "you're exhausted and under tremendous emotional stress. This person may be abusive to you on the phone. He will think he can control you more easily since you're the most vulnerable." Mary Ellen watched Nan closely as she added, "I think it would be a best to have Peter or Kathy handle the calls from the kidnapper."

Nan nodded slowly, and Mary Ellen glimpsed the keen intelligence behind the fatigue. "I see what you're saying. But won't he ask for me?" Nan looked up at her.

"Yes, he will, at least initially. But we know he expects to be dealing with a woman, so we may be able to persuade him to talk with Kathy in your place." Mary Ellen turned to Kathy. "Do you think you can do this, Kathy?"

Kathy swallowed and closed her eyes for a moment. Then she fixed a serious gaze on Mary Ellen. "I'll try, yes. If Mom wants me to. If you want me to. Oh, God, I don't know. What if I say something that hurts my dad?" She inhaled a sob, her earlier determination slowly dissolving.

"I'll be right here with you," said Mary Ellen gently. "And I'll tell you exactly what to say." She touched Kathy's shoulder. "We'll rehearse."

"Okay," Kathy said in a whisper. "I'll do it. I'll do anything for Dad." She lifted her head and pressed her lips together in a grim, determined line.

Mary Ellen continued. "Mrs. Geschke—Nan—it won't be good for you or Peter to be in the room when these calls come in. Kathy needs to be totally focused. Here's what we'll do."

She outlined her plan. After the information-gathering session on Chuck, Nan would retreat upstairs, trying to stay calm and praying her support for the others. Peter would deflect visitors to the house and type up the call scripts. For the time remaining until the phone call, Mary Ellen would coach Kathy on things to say and things to avoid saying during the phone calls. They would practice. Then, they would wait.

One thing left. Mary Ellen looked squarely at Kathy who was still sitting in a corner of the sofa, arms hugging her middle. Her posture was partly defensive, partly defiant. Mary Ellen was banking on the defiant streak.

"If the phone rings now, Kathy, before we have time to practice, you have one goal—one position to take. And that's cooperation. Let him know you're going to do whatever he says and whatever it takes to get your dad back safely. Got it?"

"All right," Kathy replied without inflection and without changing her posture.

• • •

Chuck

WITHOUT SIGHT, I was acutely aware of the smallest sound or the faintest smell. It was my only information. I was able to distinguish Rock from Steve when they approached me just by the sound of the footfall. Rock's was heavier, more deliberate. Besides, he gave me plenty of time to measure his step since he paced continuously when Steve left for a food run or a phone call. My heart raced each time Rock neared my corner, as he did now.

The toe of his shoe scraped my leg. Steve had left moments ago to get food, reminding me again not to do anything "stupid" that would make Rock mad. So I held my breath until I heard Rock's footsteps move across the room to where I guessed the kitchen was. He turned on the radio to a rock station. I exhaled.

Rock was also the sniffer, so I also tracked his proximity by the near constant, sharp uptake of his breath. The sound wrapped me in anxiety. He was probably on drugs. His judgment would be off, his emotions volatile. And Rock was the one with the gun.

It didn't help that he continued to click and release the safety on the gun, sometimes right in my ear—the same trick he had used to terrorize me from the beginning. To keep the panic from rising and to keep from throwing up with the tension, I begged God to give me a way to focus my mind on something positive. I decided to pray.

I started with the Our Father, then abandoned it for a Hail Mary. But the usual calm and comfort that prayers brought deserted me. All the years of Catholic school ... all the years of Jesuit training ... a whole lifetime of weekly mass, sometimes daily mass ... all the years of saying grace before meals and the Rosary during Lent, and I couldn't stay focused on the simplest prayers. I felt empty and alone.

Where are you, Lord? Have you abandoned me? I can't see, I can't think, I can't remember, and my prayers are hollow. What do you want me to do, Lord?

As though it were an answer, it occurred to me that my desire to pray, my turning to God, was in itself a prayer. In my confusion and fear, God was surely closer to me than ever. A small piece of calm returned. I began to breathe more deeply. Water was running in the kitchen, and the strident rock music faded into the sound.

Almost like a meditation, pictures of the children floated through my consciousness. Peter as an infant in our first little house in Cleveland, and our pure delight in him … Kathy as a ten-year-old, constantly rearranging the colors and furniture in her bedroom and anywhere else she could impose her artistic vision on us … John as a lean and handsome teenager working the copier at Adobe one summer with Kathy, magnifying fonts so we could digitize them. I dozed with my heart locked around the precious images of my children.

I figured it was late morning—today should be Wednesday—when I was jolted awake by the unmistakable jangle of chains hitting the floor. Steve was back, and Rock was again asking him if they should chain me. There was a pause. I could sense Steve standing in front of me as I sat on my sleeping bag on the floor.

He nudged me with his foot. "The rules of our organization require us to shackle you. Do you know that?"

I shook my head. "No."

"But you seem to be cooperating," Steve said. "I like that. So we leave the chains off for right now—okay? Just don't do anything stupid—okay?"

"Okay," I echoed. Was I supposed to be grateful? A tremor of anger coursed through me, but it was quickly smothered by the pervasive fear.

"And you better hope your family doesn't do anything stupid either," he said. "Or you'll end up in little pieces. You'll be shark bait. Do you hear me?" He raised his voice and lowered his body to my level. His breath was hot on my cheeks.

"Yes, yes. I hear you. They'll do whatever you say. Just tell them I said to do what you say."

"You're going to tell them yourself," said Steve, backing away from me. "You're going to make a tape, and I will play it for your wife on the phone. You will tell her to cooperate. You will tell her not to contact the authorities in any way and that your life is in her hands. Tell your family not to take any chances with your life." It sounded like he was fiddling with a machine—a tape recorder, no doubt.

Apparently satisfied that I would cooperate, Steve gave me some stock phrases he insisted that I use, like "my life is in your hands," "these people are very serious," and "follow their directions." Then he told me I could speak to my family. I heard a snap and a low whirring. "Talk," Steve ordered.

I swallowed over the rawness in my throat and fought to keep emotion and tears out of my voice. The last thing I wanted was to add to their panic. *Nan, Kathy, Peter, John, Dad ... how I love you all. Will I ever see you again?* Then, as if from a great distance, I heard my own voice, flat and heavy, but clear.

"Our lives may be in danger," I told the people I loved most in the world. "Don't gamble with my life or your own. Do what they say ... I love you very much."

The recorder clicked off, signaling the end of my message. I pulled my knees into my chest and turned toward the wall. Steve announced that he was leaving to make the phone call to Nan. The sound of the engine revving just beyond the thin wall I was leaning on roared past me like white water rushing toward falls.

• • •

Kathy

"DEEP BREATH. That's it. Another one," Mary Ellen said, and Kathy obeyed. The first ring of the phone was still lingering in the room, and Kathy was torn between an urgent desire to snatch up the receiver and an urgent desire to flee. Mary Ellen held her gaze and calmly breathed along with her in the slow rhythm they had practiced just minutes before. Then she squeezed Kathy's shoulder and nodded. Kathy reached for the phone.

Her hand was shaking. She put both hands on the receiver to steady it and prayed her voice wouldn't shake as well. But it did. "Hello?"

"May I talk to Nancy?" The slightly accented male voice was sharp and direct. It came at Kathy with the force of a blow. Reflexively, she pulled the receiver away from her ear for an instant.

Kathy swallowed into a dry throat. "Uh, she—she's sick right now. She's practically in the hospital ... this is her daughter, Kathy." Kathy looked down at the script Peter had typed and laid on the kitchen table less than half an hour ago.

Mary Ellen was close by, listening in with headphones and occasionally patting her arm for encouragement. Mary Ellen pointed to one of the phrases on the script. "Where is my dad?" it read. Kathy was reminded of her task: keep asking where Dad is. Let the kidnapper know you expect him to be alive. *God, please don't let me say anything wrong. Don't let me cause them to hurt my dad. Please, God.*

Kathy gripped the side of the table as she focused on the kidnapper's message. "Tell your mom don't do anything stupid ... she is being watched ... we know everything about you people. Anything stupid, your dad will die. Understand?" His voice level rose, became harsher. "*Do* you understand?"

"Yes, yes ... we fully intend to—anything you ... to comply with ... to ... " She lost track of her thought.

"Listen!" the caller spoke over her. "I have a message for you from your dad." Kathy inhaled sharply. There was an audible click, followed by Chuck's voice, slow and measured, without animation. Kathy shot a glance at Mary Ellen who was listening intently.

"Nan, I love you very much ... the people who have me are very serious ... follow their directions ... our lives could be in danger ..."

Dad! It was him! The tears streaming down Kathy's face at the sound of her father's voice blurred the type on the script. "Is my dad safe?" she blurted. "Is he okay?" Her voice cracked. What if they had made the tape and then shot him? What if he was bleeding? Was he suffocating in the trunk of a car by now? Kathy labored to breathe. She didn't have enough air.

Mary Ellen tightened her grip on Kathy's shoulder. Kathy locked her jaw over the hysteria that threatened to break through and somehow remained steady, frowning in concentration at the kidnapper's directions. Directions she had to get right since they could be the only way to save her father's life.

"You should have the money by June fifth. That will give you seven business days from tomorrow."

Mary Ellen tapped a phrase on the paper.

"Uh—um, can we get him earlier than that?" Kathy interrupted. "Like tomorrow? If I can have the money ready by tomorrow?"

"Then I'll call you tomorrow," the kidnapper said brusquely and went on with his instructions. "If you have the money, you will make the drop for me. Nobody else. You will use your mom's Jaguar. Do you understand me?"

"Okay." Kathy's breathing was uneven with the strain of concentration. Why the Jaguar? Had they marked it? Put a bomb in it?

"And make sure nobody knows ... "

In that instant, the irony overcame her, and she forgot caution. "Who's gonna know except me, you, and my mother?" she blurted. There was an edge of sarcasm in Kathy's voice. She was wearing thin, getting angry. Worse, she had strayed from the script. She looked at Mary Ellen. The agent was smiling.

The caller continued. "I don't want your brother ... in New Jersey to find out. I don't want Peter to find out, either. I'm very serious

… anything happens you're all going—I mean, something's going to happen to your dad. You're all gonna be sorry."

Kathy took another risk. "Can I talk to my dad?"

"No. He's not in this state. He's not in California."

"How do I know he's safe?"

"Once we have the money, he'll be released after twelve hours."

"Are you sure I can't talk to him?" Mary Ellen kept nodding as Kathy continued to press.

"No. I'll call you tomorrow."

The kidnapper hung up. Kathy stared straight ahead, seeing nothing. She still gripped the phone.

"It's over, Kathy," Mary Ellen said quietly. "You were wonderful. Absolutely perfect. You kept him on the line longer than we hoped, so the trace should be easier. And you got him off center, Kathy. Your questions took some of the control away from him without his realizing it. We couldn't ask for anything more."

As Mary Ellen continued to praise her, Kathy slowly crumpled into a ball on the kitchen chair, damp with perspiration and wet with tears. "I can't do this! I can't do this!" she whispered. Her neck was so rigid, she could barely turn her head.

Mary Ellen stood over Kathy's chair from behind, both arms on her shoulders, reminding her over and over what a strong advantage she was to her dad and how much she had accomplished for the FBI, even though she didn't realize it. Gradually, Kathy's breathing evened out. She stood, and some of the tension drained from her shoulders. Then she allowed Mary Ellen to lead her to the family room sofa where she immediately fell asleep.

· EVENING ·

Nan

ABOUT FIVE O'CLOCK, Marva came back with several large containers of Chinese chicken salad from Chef Chu's, the favorite take-out place for both our families. Kathy was still sleeping, and I was in the family room with Peter praying the Rosary when Marva tiptoed in from the back door. The familiar aroma of our favorite Chinese food almost lured me into believing it was just another weekend dinner with John and Marva and whichever of our kids happened to wander in and out.

But when I heard Chuck's easy laughter in my head, the reality came back, and tears with it. I wondered what Chuck was eating tonight— or if he was eating at all. Suddenly, the idea of eating a meal with family and friends in our homey kitchen seemed absurd. I couldn't. I gave Marva a quick hug and went back upstairs for a cigarette as she and Peter began setting out the plates.

Standing in the bathroom connected to our bedroom, I looked out over the backyard, periodically and deliberately blurring my own vision with a long exhale of smoke directed upward over my eyes. I didn't want to see what I saw: black-jacketed strangers patrolling our grounds, obviously armed; federal agents changing shifts, entering and exiting through our back door. Fortunately for us, the house sat next to the entry path for a Los Altos nature park, so cars turning into the little road would appear to be visiting the park rather than detouring into our backyard. Anyone watching the front of the house would miss all the activity in the rear. At least that was our hope.

I put down the lid cover and sat on the toilet. Chuck would hate it if he knew I was smoking. How I longed to hear his annoyance—to listen to him fume and growl about how the smoke would ruin my health and seep into the upholstery and— My eyes filled as I conjured up the familiar inflections of his voice. My hand shook as the column of ash grew longer.

What did God want of me? It had been seven years now since my sister Kathy had been killed—no, murdered. None of us—probably not even the courts—had believed it really was involuntary manslaughter when Kathy's estranged and deranged husband shot her that night in a supposed tussle over a gun. But tricks of the law and a flashy defense had managed to change murder into manslaughter. The thought of it still made me tremble with outrage.

And here I was again: trembling, weeping, disoriented, sliding into depression and panic, on the brink of losing my husband, my life's partner, my greatest love—losing him to murder! *What do you want of me, God?*

After Kathy's death, I would wonder over and over how my sweet sister had found herself in a situation that was so far beyond our experience, or even our imagination. I never was able to answer how or why violence had penetrated our ordinary, comfortable lives. We had grown up so sheltered and safe in our big, close Irish Catholic family, no strangers to bickering and disappointment, but worlds away from crime and fear. Yet here I was again.

All my life I had been taught to trust in God's plan, to live the life that was before me, to pray to know and accept God's will for me. Maybe that faith ritual had sustained me through my sister's death and the painful anger and depression that followed.

Maybe the seed of faith was planted so deeply that, angry or not, fearful or not, it sustained me, even though I thought God had abandoned me at the time. There was something indefinable and powerful at my core that would not allow me to give up hope. *I don't understand, God. But I trust.*

A car door slammed, and I returned to the window. John Warnock was jogging through the yard to the back door. Two agents were with him. He might have news from Adobe. I dropped the cigarette into the toilet bowl, flushed, and went downstairs to rejoin the group in the kitchen.

• • •

The Warnocks

MARVA WARNOCK was annoyed by the FBI. They had politely declined to eat the food yesterday at her house and still they refused, despite the fact that she had brought enough for an army of agents. They didn't want to be any trouble, they told her. The result was a trail of McDonald's take-out bags winding through the house at all hours.

Nor did Peter eat much. "My stomach keeps churning," he said, apologizing. "And my allergies are so bad right now that I can't taste anything." He helped Marva cover the plates with aluminum foil. "Maybe later." He sighed heavily and began to cough. Marva looked at Peter's eyes, nearly swollen shut and watery—whether from his lingering cold or real tears, she couldn't tell.

John Warnock came in the back door just as Nan was entering the kitchen. He hugged her wordlessly and led her to a chair at the kitchen table. Marva unwrapped a container of chicken salad and pulled two plates from the cupboard for Nan and John.

"What's happening at Adobe?" Nan asked John. "Do they know about Chuck? Are they asking questions?"

"I've already called Clinton and Stephen," John said, naming two of the senior managers he and Chuck relied on. "We agreed not to say anything to the employees in general. The FBI doesn't want the news spreading either. Only on a need-to-know basis. Some folks are beginning to notice, though. They're asking when Chuck will be back in the office."

"With the FBI crawling around the place, no wonder they're suspicious," said Peter shaking his head.

"Probably true," said John, "because they weren't very subtle."

"Like watching the house with all the lights on and black jackets streaming in and out the front door," said Nan, reminding them of the scene last midnight when she and Agent Taylor had arrived at the house. "The complete opposite of subtle," she said wryly.

John went on, "The agents had me pull in a few folks who worked closely with Chuck. Then they grilled us about any employees who had a beef with Adobe in general or Chuck in particular—you know, people who had left, people who were terminated, people who'd been reprimanded. But there just wasn't a likely candidate, no matter how hard we racked our brains. Have to say the agents were thorough."

John passed a hand over his face, remembering his personal grilling from the FBI the night before. For two hours straight, they had questioned him about his relationship with Chuck, about the state of the business, about Nan and Chuck's marriage, about the Geschke kids, about the Warnock kids, about their friends, even—for heaven's sake—about whether Nan and Chuck might have conspired to stage this crime themselves, for God only knows what reason.

It was clear to John Warnock that the FBI was still working on the assumption that the kidnapping was an inside job, with a connection to either family, friends, or Adobe. That theory didn't add up for John. He knew in his soul it wasn't. He had believed it was the real thing from the moment he read Nan's desperate note outside Rancho Market.

"They have to turn over every rock," said Peter. "Their job. Me, I'm the computer guy now. I monitor Dad's bank accounts for activity and type up the call transcripts for them to analyze. When I'm not on the computer, I'm saying the Rosary nonstop with Mom. Calms us both down, right, Mom?" Peter gave Nan a gentle jab with his elbow, extracting a small smile as reward.

"What happens when they decide none of us or none of the Adobe employees are potential suspects?" Marva said, leaving the littered countertop to join them at the table. "What's next?"

"For one thing, they'll play the tape of today's call for the group at Adobe, see if the voice jogs a memory for someone," answered John.

Peter said, "They had language experts here listening to the tape, too. Mary Ellen told me they were having some trouble identifying the accent. They're thinking it's Middle Eastern, but they're not certain."

The chicken salad, Cokes, and coffee gradually dwindled as the little group absently snacked and speculated about possible suspects and motives, coming up maddeningly short. Chuck had few, if any, known enemies.

"Why him, do you think?" asked Marva. "There are dozens of business owners and executives here in the Valley—lots of them with more money than the Adobe people." Then something struck her. "Oh! You know what?" The others waited for her brainstorm. "There was a picture and article in the paper a few weeks ago about Nan's giving a major donation to San Jose State University."

"I remember the article," said Nan. "We gave some money to the school of library science. Sort of a thank-you for my graduate degree from there. They could have gotten our connection to Adobe from that."

"True," said John. "Also, the *Mercury* publishes an annual list of Valley executive salaries. That came out a couple of months ago." He chuckled briefly. "That used to annoy the hell out of Chuck."

Peter stood and crossed into the kitchen, reaching for the coffeepot. He returned to the table and refilled the cups. "How do you think they came up with such a weird sum of money?" he asked as he poured. "Come on, man, who asks for $650,000 when you could just as easily ask for a million?"

"I thought about that, and oddly enough, that's the same amount of Adobe's quarterly tax estimate," said John. "But how on earth could they know that?"

Nan answered, "If they were really snooping around the house, they could have seen it written on the notepad on Chuck's desk. I saw it there myself before I left for Russia. It was right next to the window wall in the ground-floor office."

Marva shuddered. "Dear God, can you imagine them creeping around the backyard, looking in your windows?"

"I can imagine them doing anything to get money," said a scornful, dispirited voice floating toward them from the hall. Kathy came into the kitchen. They all turned toward her, and John pulled out a chair.

"Come on, eat with us, honey," he said.

Kathy sat but didn't eat. "Tell me what happened at Adobe," she said to John immediately, preempting their questions about the phone call. But Pete spoke up, and she smiled at her brother's glowing report of Mary Ellen's glowing report of her handling of the negotiations with the kidnappers. She didn't volunteer anything more.

"Of all five Geschkes," Pete said with conviction, "Kathy is by far our best frontline manager. She just, you know, takes charge." He grinned at his sister with affection. "She can handle stuff."

THURSDAY | MAY 28

· MORNING ·

FBI

AS THEY PREPARED for the next ransom call expected in the afternoon, Mary Ellen and the agents on duty at the Geschke home allowed themselves to feel a little positive. Kathy had kept the kidnapper on the line long enough yesterday to trace the call to the vicinity of Hollister, a community of twenty-some thousand about sixty miles south of Los Altos. It was a good bet that Mr. Geschke was well hidden in one of the many farming towns in the heart of garlic and artichoke country. The Bureau didn't believe he'd been taken across the border.

Time wasn't on their side. Every hour that went by without action or information lessened Mr. Geschke's chances of survival. But Mary Ellen didn't repeat that theory to Nan and Kathy and Peter. Their pallid faces and haunted eyes proved they already knew it.

The more she worked with these people, the more Mary Ellen admired them. In her experience, the individual and joint stress they were forced to endure made most families of victims dissolve into accusations and shouting matches. Old family wounds would often rise to the surface, bleeding anew. Sometimes, even the agents and officers working a case would be targets of a family's anger, frustration, and downright abuse. Tension and fear made people vicious.

But not this family. Not even close. Mary Ellen's studies in human behavior suggested that the Geschkes were not typical in coping with personal anguish. They talked little. Mostly, they prayed. Quietly and steadily, they prayed. Together and alone, they prayed.

Even in the midst of their fear and helplessness, Mary Ellen noted unusual unity and unusual strength. Like Peter's trips upstairs to check on his mother, his "third ear" tuned in to her frame of mind. Like Kathy's determined study of the scripts, her focus on getting it right, even anticipating questions and suggesting answers herself.

About midmorning, Mary Ellen and Kathy settled at the dining room table to rehearse possible scenarios for the day's promised phone call.

"What if he asks for my mom again?" Kathy asked.

"I really doubt he will. He seems okay about working with you," answered Mary Ellen. "But if he does, talk about her poor health and how badly this is affecting the whole family. Ask about your dad's physical condition. Tell him your health is being affected, too. We want to pressure him, make him feel responsible for your lives as well as your dad's."

Kathy nodded, following carefully and deep in thought.

Mary Ellen continued, "As often as you can, repeat that you and your family fully intend to comply with all his demands. Assure him you're going to cooperate."

"That will help my dad, right?"

"Definitely. It will. If they believe they're getting away with this easily, there's no reason to add to their crime by hurting their hostage. They begin congratulating themselves on how clever they are and become more likely to slip up." Mary Ellen thought of something and stopped to make a note on the script.

She went on. "And keep asking how your dad is—if he's safe, if you can talk to him, when you're going to see him," she said.

"What do I say about the money?"

"Tell him you have it, that you're ready to—"

"But I *don't!* It was supposed to be here by now! What if he tells me to come right after he calls me?" Kathy stood up jerkily, toppling the chair behind her.

"Don't worry, it will be." Mary Ellen was less certain than she sounded. The task of assembling and marking more than six thousand separate bills in one day was daunting. She knew they were scrambling back at the San Francisco headquarters.

Kathy and Mary Ellen spent the remainder of the morning listing and role-playing possible questions and answers. Kathy had clear goals to achieve in each phone call. Mary Ellen instructed her to ask if a courier could be used to make the drop. It was unlikely the kidnapper would agree, but the Bureau wanted to try anything that might remove Kathy from a role that would expose her to potential violence.

The next best scenario would be to conceal an agent in the car with Kathy as she made the drop. But the kidnapper—probably to prove he had indeed followed them and knew their cars—had insisted that Kathy use her mother's Jaguar. Hiding an agent in the back of the Jaguar was impossible. Somehow Kathy had to steer him to another option.

"Insist on using your parents' Cadillac," Mary Ellen told her. "The only way we'll let you deliver the money is if you have an armed agent on the floor behind you. It's critical, Kathy."

"Oh, God. What if I can't change his mind? What if he won't agree? Then what do I do?" Kathy was agitated, shaky again.

Mary Ellen watched her closely. What a burden to put on this girl! No matter how strong and sophisticated she looked, at twenty-four years old she was still extremely young, a daughter, with the fate of a beloved parent riding on her shoulders. Still, there was something in her that Mary Ellen instinctively trusted: a steely core of anger and nerve that occasionally flared beneath the fear.

Mary Ellen said, "Kathy, you've been awesome so far. Keep doing what you're doing. You're engaging him in just the right way."

"But I'm so scared," whispered Kathy. "I'm scared I'm going to lose it on the phone, and he'll hang up and do something to my dad. I'm so scared of that, Mary Ellen."

Mary Ellen nodded her understanding. Though much of her professional life was spent with the most hardened and disturbed of criminals—perhaps partly because of that—Mary Ellen was perceptive and sympathetic to people's pain. Especially the pain of victims. And there was no doubt this brave young woman was a victim in every sense. Mary Ellen reached for Kathy's hand and turned slightly away so that Kathy wouldn't see the sorrow brimming in her eyes.

• • •

Kathy

THE MORNING DRAGGED toward noon, and Kathy began to worry about Grandpa Matt. Chuck's father, Matthew Geschke, now ninety, had lived with them until last year when he had moved to an assisted living apartment close by. Chuck, Nan, or one of the kids either visited or called him every day.

"What should we do about Grandpa, Mom? We've got to let him know *something*," said Kathy. She and Nan and Pete had gathered in the master bedroom to talk.

"He'll really be confused if he doesn't hear from one of us today," said Peter. "No one has talked to him since the party on Monday."

"I know, I know," said Nan, fingering her rosary beads. "And John. We've got to keep him from asking questions when he calls." Nan frowned in concentration.

Kathy admired her mother's effort to stay focused and calm. She was involved yet distant. It was unlike Nan to back away and let others take charge, but this time she seemed relieved. Kathy couldn't imagine the anxiety her mother was feeling, even though her own fear had invaded every aspect of her being. Every time the phone rang, her heart hammered ferociously against her ribs and her breathing turned shallow. How many times had Mary Ellen whispered during yesterday's phone call, "Slow down, Kathy. Breathe, Kathy"?

And the phone rang steadily. The few Adobe managers that knew the situation wanted to help however they could. John Warnock called regularly to check on them. The hardest were the calls from her friends. Kathy would answer every call, heart pounding and ears ringing. Upon hearing the familiar voice of a friend, it was all she could do to prevent a cry of relief, which was instantly replaced with wariness and a supreme effort to sound natural—which, of course, made her sound unnatural.

When she canceled plans for a long-awaited spa visit with two friends, she could tell they were suspicious. How could Kathy—who was always ready for any adventure, who was rarely sick or even tired—how could she be so sick that she would cancel plans they'd talked about for ages? Something's up, they accused. What's going on? Her misery with the need to deceive her friends was overpowered by her fear that they might find out and somehow compromise her dad's life. She continued to deceive them.

"It will be hard to fool Grandpa Matt in a phone call," Nan said at last. "How about a fax?"

"Fax might be better; the FBI doesn't really want us to call anyone. Especially John. They don't want him to get suspicious," Kathy replied to her mom.

"Yeah. It creates another variable they can't control," Peter said.

"They may still think he's involved," said Nan wryly. "They suspected me for hours that first night. They suspected you and your friends for a while, too. I know they have to focus on the family first. But to keep John completely removed feels wrong ... like he's not a part of the family."

The phone rang. Kathy raced downstairs to meet Mary Ellen in the kitchen.

"It's too early, isn't it?" breathed Kathy.

"I think so," said Mary Ellen. "Sit and take a couple of deep breaths before you pick up."

She got it just before the fourth ring. Finally, it was John, the call she'd been both hoping for and dreading. "John! What's up?" Kathy tried to sound casual and energetic at the same time, while glancing to Mary Ellen in near panic. Surely her own brother would be able to detect the phoniness in her voice.

He did. "Geez, you sound weird. What's going on? What are you doing home, anyway? Aren't you supposed to be nonstop job-hunting? Or are you going to sponge off Mom and Dad for the rest of your life?"

John's familiar sibling banter relaxed her a little. Kathy had never wished harder that she could tell her younger brother how much she loved him. The emotion took her by surprise and made her eyes well up. Mary Ellen touched her arm lightly. Kathy was grateful for the silent support.

She gave her brother a light laugh. "Wish I could. Actually, just visiting. You know, um—wedding stuff with Mom and Pete and Diane."

"Oh, yeah. *The-e-e* wedding. Is Mom there?"

"Um, yeah. But, ah … she can't talk. She's sick."

"Oh no. Bad? Not sleeping? One of her hyperanxiety deals?"

"No, no, no. Nothing like that," Kathy said quickly. Too quickly.

"Then why can't she talk? Where is she?" There was a hint of annoyance in his voice.

"She's sleeping, that's all. After the Russia trip, she was super-exhausted and she caught this really bad cold. Actually she's got laryngitis and the doctor told her not to talk at all for a few days." Kathy felt the lameness in her story.

"Hey, she'll talk to me, no matter what. I'm 'the baby,' you know! Okay, I'll try to call her back. In the meantime, I'll call Dad at the office to check in."

"Well, uh—Dad's out of town, John." Kathy glanced over at Mary Ellen who was listening to their conversation on the headphones.

Mary Ellen made a thumbs-up sign, but John wasn't buying it.

"Kathy, come on, level with me. You don't sound normal. Is something going on with Mom and Dad? Marriage problems? Good God, are they going to get a divorce or something? Is that what you're keeping from me?" He sounded both angry and anxious.

"Oh, be serious. If it was something like that, I'd be calling *you*!" Kathy attempted to sound offhand, her face crumpling as she spoke. "So. What's happening there?"

"Getting ready for the big campout with my roommates," he said. "Finals are over, and we are *out of here*." John punched the last three words with a ringing laugh.

Kathy was grateful for his excitement and preoccupation with his senior week plans. His Princeton graduation was less than two weeks off, and it was doubtful that some distant confusion at home would override his high spirits and big plans to celebrate.

"That's why I need to talk to Mom and Dad," he went on. "We'll be in the woods, totally unreachable for a few days."

"I'll let everyone know. Call us as soon as you get back. Have a great time—and don't do anything I wouldn't do." Kathy tried to force a smile into her voice.

"Yeah, sure. Thanks." John still seemed puzzled as he hung up, but Kathy was overcome with relief that the conversation was over.

She began to cry quietly. "I wanted to tell him so bad. I feel rotten for lying to him like that," she said to Mary Ellen. "It's not as if he doesn't suspect something's wrong," she added defensively.

Mary Ellen was sympathetic, but reminded her, "Your little lies might be saving his life, Kathy. We don't know yet what we're dealing with. We have to assume that you're all in danger."

Kathy nodded. "Yeah. I get it," she sniffed.

After the challenging conversation with her brother, Kathy understood why Mary Ellen and the other agents wanted to minimize phone contact with family and friends. She, Pete, her mom, and Mary Ellen decided that Kathy should fax Grandpa Geschke the laryngitis story, praying he would buy it. Peter developed a message that would make sense to their grandfather and typed it in a large, boldface font:

Grandpa,
Mom and Peter are sick with strep throat and
are very contagious. I am staying here at the
house to take care of them. One of us will come
to see you when we aren't contagious anymore.
Please fax me back to say that you're okay.
Kathy

Still troubled by having to deceive her family, Kathy slowly dialed the fax number for Grandpa Matt. They were already isolated from Chuck; they had to isolate John with their awkward pretense; they had built a protective shell around Nan; they had lied to their friends; even Pete was somewhat removed from her, caught up in the work of the FBI agents. And now they were forced to keep Grandpa at a distance—Grandpa, who loved them all so openly and joyfully.

Dad, why is everyone safe but you and me? You must feel all alone, too. I'm trying to build that boat to get you off the island, but it's hard, Dad. And I'm scared. I'm scared to let you down and ...

An unbidden memory flooded Kathy's vision, triggered by the words "let you down." A geometry test when she was a sophomore in high school. How she hated geometry! The only thing worse was doing geometry homework with Dad. The nightly tutoring sessions were agony for both of them. But Chuck was convinced she would get it—eventually.

After all, look at her heritage! Her dad, a whisper away from a PhD in math, had a PhD in computer science. No difference as far as Kathy was concerned. She was the only daughter of a math wizard, and she was hopeless. Her thought patterns sprang and skipped and circled, refusing to march in orderly shapes and columns. Kathy didn't particularly mind, but her dad did, and that made all the difference.

Kathy had rallied to her dad's faith in her and studied geometry harder and longer than any other subject that year. She strained and tensed over each problem. She *willed* herself to get it—mostly to please her dad. The whole week before an especially important test, Chuck had tutored and she had practiced—but to no avail. She remembered bringing home her D, or maybe it was an F. Seeing the disappointment in her dad's face, despite his attempt to brush past it and encourage her, had made Kathy wilt with sorrow.

She smiled at the power of the memory. Miserable as she was, she had known even then that her dad's pride and delight in her had never wavered. As an adult, she was perfectly secure in the great gift of her father's respect. But today, warring with all the other emotions swirling in her head and heart, her childish fear of disappointing him returned to haunt her. She pressed her index fingers into the corners of her eyes to thwart the welling tears.

I won't fail the test this time, Dad. I promise. I'm scared for my-self. I hope you're praying for me. I'm sticking with you, Dad. Wait for me.

• • •

Chuck

THEY BROUGHT ME something from McDonald's again for breakfast this morning. One of the McMuffin things: ham, egg, and cheese. My senses of smell and taste were by now so acute that I knew what it was from the minute Steve parked the car near the outside door. Simple deduction also helped, I suppose, since McDonald's had been my only food source for the past two days.

While I ate, Steve and Rock watched a part of some movie on TV. I couldn't follow this one. Last night, they had watched *Ghost*, a movie I remembered seeing. Catching a familiar line here or there or imagining the details of a certain scene had been strangely comforting as I listened to the action while staring into the black fabric of my blindfold.

When the movie ended, they let me use the bathroom. Rock stood just outside the door, which he hadn't pulled completely closed behind me. After I flushed the toilet, I stood for a long time at the narrow sink, anointing my hands with cool running water, wishing powerfully that I could splash my face and my parched, burning eyes.

Settled back in my corner again, I had no concept of the time, except that it still must be morning. Rock bent over me and tightened my blindfold. I could not open my eyes completely, but if I pushed them hard against the fabric, I could see some grayish light from the bottom rim. No shapes. As Rock moved away from me, he kicked at the chains lying on the floor. As before, I jerked at the sudden noisy clanking by my side. He laughed. "Elephant chains," he chortled. "Do anything stupid and we put you in elephant chains."

From the opposite side of the room, Steve said, "So far, your family, they're good. They're cooperating okay."

"I know they'll do whatever you ask," I said. "We all will." I couldn't imagine the weight of stress Nan and Kathy were enduring at home. I hoped Peter was with them and prayed that John was still safe at school. *Protect them all, Lord.* It seemed important that I help keep my captors calm, that I assure them their plan would work. They sounded proud that things were working so far, even a little cocky. I was terrified of what they might do if something went wrong.

"We invested a lot of money in this plan." Steve's voice came to me from farther away. Was there a kitchen somewhere? The house wasn't large at all, judging by the opening and closing of the front door that sounded pretty close to me. And the garage, where Rock had gone to lift weights yesterday afternoon, was only eight or ten steps in the other direction. I had heard Rock straining and grunting as plainly as though he were in the next room.

There was some tearing paper and a snapping of something like hard plastic from the direction of Steve's voice—as though a package was being opened. "We have planned very smart," Steve said. He then described, to my absolute amazement, a bizarre escape plan which involved spiriting the money away from the pickup point in a one-man submarine under the waters of Monterey Bay!

"We have one of the torpedoes off the submarine," Steve continued with an unmistakable note of pride. "Want to feel it?"

Incredulous as I was, I said, "Sure," hoping to sound appropriately enthusiastic.

He pulled my hand along the side of a smooth, bullet-shaped object about two or three feet long. "From a thirty-five thousand dollar submarine, man!" he said.

"Wow." I kept running my hand along the object. "Sure feels like a torpedo to me. Really impressive," I said. From the size and shape, I judged it to be part of a one-man, self-propelled dive suit. I'd seen such a contraption once or twice on beachgoers in wet suits.

Could this be Steve's "submarine"? Did he think I'd believe any real submarine would cost only thirty-five thousand dollars? If so, why did it take so many billions to fund the U.S. Navy? In that brief moment, I believed that God was sending a little comedy to distract and calm me. It helped for a while.

I get it, Lord. You're reminding me to keep trusting in you, right? You're telling me you're right here with me. I believe you. I'll never stop believing you.

Apparently satisfied with my admiration of his getaway plan, Steve packed away the torpedo and announced it was time to get ready for the next phone call to Kathy. I heard something clatter against a hard surface, followed by a snap or lock, two rapid clicks, and then a whirring sound. Of course, the tape recorder. He was going to record me again for the phone call.

Something occurred to me, and I decided it was time to take a small chance. They might buy into the idea. "How will they know I'm alive?" I asked Steve offhandedly from my corner. "What point is there in getting the money for you if they don't know for sure I'm alive?"

"The tape. We will play the tape of your voice. They positively know it is you," Steve said.

"But you could have taped me yesterday ... or the day before. They have no way of knowing I'm not already dead," I said calmly, knowing the logic was bound to get through—to Steve, at least.

From the hiccup of silence I perceived on an intake of breath somewhere across from me, I realized that in all his astute planning, Steve had not considered the one thing that might cause my family to withhold the money. I was positive Nan would never play odds like that with my life. Absolutely positive. But Steve and Rock couldn't be sure. I had uncovered a crack in the wall of their master plan—a crack I could wedge open to my advantage.

"They need definite proof I'm alive before they can get this money together," I hedged. "For instance, you could tell me the front-page headline on this morning's *Mercury*, and I could recite it to them."

I knew Steve had picked up a newspaper with breakfast for the past two days. After ten minutes of paper-rustling and page-turning, Steve had announced that there were no stories about a kidnapping in Los Altos. I could tell they were pleased. They thought they were controlling the progression of events. They probably were.

Still, heartened by the chance to get encouraging information to my family, I pressed on. "If they hear those words in my voice and check the paper, it will prove that I'm alive—today, at least."

Steve and Rock conferred. Steve didn't see any downside for them, which there wasn't, and understood the benefit. Rock was suspicious. "He's not the boss. He can't tell us what to do," he argued. It was all about muscle as far as Rock was concerned.

"You want the money, don't you?" Steve snapped back. "The

daughter is always asking where is her dad, is he safe, is he okay, can she talk to him—all the time on the phone. So what's the matter proving he's okay if it keeps them cooperating?"

Rock didn't argue anymore. They would use my plan. Despite my unrelenting fear of something going wrong, I felt a glimmer of satisfaction. They had listened to *me*. It amazed me what importance I attached to such a miniscule crumb of control.

When the machine was set to record, Steve repeated his instructions from the day before. "Just tell them not to do anything stupid. Tell them to do exactly what we say and you'll be okay." Steve read me a headline: "'San Francisco judge strikes down abortion consent law.'" Then he snapped down the record button.

I steeled my voice to keep emotion at bay and recorded the message to my loved ones, trying to picture each of them safe in our house. When Steve left to make the call, I huddled against the wall in my corner and tried to soothe myself by praying my improvised version of the Rosary. The rhythm of the recurring Hail Mary against the backdrop of thudding barbells in the garage where Rock was lifting weights pulled me into an uneasy sleep.

· AFTERNOON ·

Nan

AFTER THEY SENT the fax, the kids and I lunched on cheese and crackers. The agents kept to the other room—usually two or three of them in addition to Mary Ellen. I didn't bother to follow their shift changes anymore. All that mattered to us—to Kathy, especially—was that Mary Ellen was there. And she was—around the clock, leaving for only brief intervals to change clothes or catch a nap. When she left, a female agent was always close by. I'm convinced the male agents didn't want to deal with me since I literally chased them out the first night, and I still had no regrets given the circumstances!

The tension of waiting was in the air, and nobody said much. The phone sat on the kitchen counter like a prized artifact on display: *Chuck's lifeline.* When Kathy and Peter began to play cards at the kitchen table, I trudged back upstairs to my room—*our* room. *Was my subconscious already accepting a life without Chuck?*

The lure of the cigarettes waiting for me on the bathroom sink was strong. I squelched the thought that someday I'd have to go through the pain of quitting all over again. It seemed irrelevant now. Besides, I felt superfluous. Kathy was the key player now, totally tuned in to Mary Ellen's mentoring and the anticipated phone calls. Peter was being the rock his name implies, helping the FBI with the scripts and computer access to Chuck's personal files and accounts. He was also doing food runs and other errands for the agents. There was no job for me but to stay out of the way and support them all.

Everyone was solicitous of me, but I could sense the relief each time I announced I was going upstairs to read or pray or nap. Couldn't blame them, really. I simply couldn't handle anything more than I had on the first day. Not only had my body given up, my mind—my soul—felt raw and desolate. I had used up every reserve of strength. I wanted only to smoke and sleep. When I couldn't do either, I prayed.

Thank you, God, for the gift of belief in prayer. I believe that you understand our fears and hear our cries . . . I have always believed that you give us the strength we need to get through life's hardships. But I honestly don't know about this one, Lord. We've been taught to have faith in your plan for each of us. But don't ask any more of us—please don't! Please, please make it your plan to bring Chuck back to us.

Absorbed in my conversation with God, I momentarily forgot about the cigarettes. I sat on the edge of the bed and reached for my rosary on the nightstand. I was disheartened and close to tears again. Leaning back against the pillows, I half-lay, half-sat, with one leg straight on the bed in front of me and the other dangling over the side. In a matter of minutes, the rhythm of the Hail Marys, ten in a row, began to quiet my jumbled thoughts.

It wasn't just the cadence that was soothing, though. It was the tradition. I had prayed the Rosary and similar prayers with my family since kindergarten—maybe even before that. I silently thanked my parents for building my trust in God and my belief in prayer. How could I get through this—or anything difficult—without my faith? Had we provided our own children with the same solid foundation? I fervently hoped so.

There was little noise from downstairs. Either my constant state of stress-born fatigue, my tranquilizers, or both created a thin curtain of fog in my head that made voices and traffic and household noise seem distant. I let my mind wander, hoping I could block out the sound of the phone when it rang ... block out the thought of my daughter's fear when I could do nothing to help.

Nor could I tolerate the thought of Chuck's being hurt or tormented or afraid. Fortunately, the sleepy dullness in my brain didn't allow me to focus on anything for too long. But Chuck's image never left me. It was as if I were holding his hand and we were walking through parts of our past together. I stretched, got up, and wandered into the bathroom for a cigarette. I blew smoke at the bathroom window and stood for a while looking through the thin, grayish cloud.

I could see us all so clearly sitting family council–style around our breakfast table all those evenings in the early '80s when Chuck was thinking about leaving Xerox and starting Adobe with John Warnock. His parents, Matt and Sophie, were often there with us. Chuck was excited about the work he and John were doing—and frustrated to no end with the corporate red tape at Xerox that was slowing and restraining them. We talked endlessly about the pros and cons.

The Xerox job was a good one, and our cautious, responsible side saw the risk in leaving the comfort zone. We had hit our stride. Chuck was an executive with a good salary and good benefits. College for all three kids was assured. Our future seemed secure. Materially speaking, our life was exactly what we had studied and worked and hoped for. Spiritually, too, we had been gifted beyond measure: a stable marriage, responsible children, a deep faith, strong family ties, meaningful work.

But Chuck was becoming more and more unhappy. He had so much to contribute! He thought Xerox was too conservative, too indecisive about investing in new technologies. "We'll lose our window of opportunity very soon," he would say. "What do you think, Nan? Is it too much risk? What if things don't work out?" He listed the potential pitfalls.

But I already knew what we would do, what we should do. "Things always work out," I told him calmly. "If we don't at least try this, you'll always be dissatisfied at some level. You know you will."

"Probably true," Chuck said. He had given me the boyish half-grin that always worked on my heart. "You know me too well." I swallowed hard, remembering the look of absolute love and respect and understanding we had exchanged at that moment.

Besides, we agreed, Chuck was well-trained, well-experienced, and had an excellent professional reputation in the Valley. He'd have little trouble finding a job if our gamble didn't work.

So we went for it. And it did work—beyond our wildest dreams. It also put us in the situation we were facing at the moment. I lifted the lid and dropped my tiny stub of cigarette into the toilet. I drew a long, shaky breath and blew it out through my mouth, hoping to rid my lungs of at least some of the poison I was feeding them.

On the end of my exhale, the phone rang so imperiously that I gulped in air. That would be our call—the one that might determine whether my husband lived or died, the call that would demand all the strength and will and intelligence our daughter possessed. *Chuck! Kathy! Protect them, Lord.* I quietly mouthed "Hail Mary, full of grace" as I fumbled for a cigarette.

• • •

Kathy
"Hello?"

"Is this Kathy?

"Yes. Who's this?" Kathy clamped one hand on the other to keep the receiver from shaking. Mary Ellen adjusted her headset and put her arm around Kathy's shoulders.

"I'm the person who called you yesterday about your dad. Now listen! I got a tape for you, a new tape that proves your dad is still alive."

"Okay." Kathy was having trouble breathing. Mary Ellen nodded encouragement.

"Get a piece of paper and a pen so you can record some stuff."

"Okay. I'm ready," Kathy said. Her telephone arm was shaking violently now.

"Now listen very carefully ... uh ... "

"I don't hear anything!" Kathy began to hyperventilate again. There was a moment of silence followed by faint static.

Then Chuck's voice: "Kathy, to show you that this tape is being made today, which is Thursday, the headline in the morning *San Jose Mercury News* says 'San Francisco judge strikes down abortion consent law.'

"I'm very sorry you're in this position that we all are. But you have to realize that my life is in your hands, and I ask you not to gamble with it, or with your own. These people are very serious, and they have sophisticated equipment.

"I know they're asking you to withdraw money. Please follow their directions. Don't contact the authorities. They really don't want us to jeopardize our lives or the lives of anyone that we love. Again, I'm very sorry that you have to deal with this. I love you both very much. I can't wait to see you again."

At the sound of her father's voice, Kathy began crying uncontrollably. Her body shook and slumped in the chair. Mary Ellen strengthened her grip on Kathy's shoulders and literally pulled her into an upright position at the table, allowing Kathy to lean into her for support.

"Did you hear that?" the caller barked out.

Kathy's voice wavered, "Is my d—my dad's okay?" Mary Ellen tapped her pen on the script. Kathy looked down at the paper and then added, "Is there a way I can talk to him?"

The caller talked over her question. "Now you listen to me very, very, very carefully. When you draw that kind of money from the banks or ... "

Kathy broke in quickly and clearly. "The money is all set."

"When you get the money, make sure you're not followed by anybody. Anybody who follows you, that means you're in trouble, your dad is in trouble ... "

"The money is ready—" Mary Ellen gave Kathy an urgent signal to read a line from the script. Kathy glanced at the paper. "—but I won't be able to get it until eight o'clock this evening. They're trying to put it all together."

"How is that possible? Your dad had eighty thousand dollars in his checking, fifty thousand dollars in his savings, plus ... " The caller sounded annoyed, agitated.

Kathy's argumentative side briefly overtook her shakiness. "It takes a while to get that kind of money ... and I had to get it all in one hundred dollar bills. They assured me it would be all ready for me and—"

"Who? Who assured you? Who assured you?"

Kathy looked at Mary Ellen in near panic, then plunged on. "The people, the money, the people my mom talked to and uh, Alex Brown at the uh—the bank."

"Wait, wait, wait. Slow down. Slow down ... we know everything about your dad and what he has. Who did you contact to get that money?"

Mary Ellen's smile signaled her that the alarm in the kidnapper's question and his willingness to stay on the phone were good. Kathy had thrown him a curve ball with the name "Alex Brown." She had nibbled a slight edge off his control of the situation. She felt a little jolt of power that passed in an instant.

"My dad's stockbroker, Alex Brown."

"Good." The caller sounded satisfied with her answer. "Now we'll call you—"

Kathy blurted through a fresh wave of tears in her voice, "My mom isn't—we're not—"

"Listen!" Loud and imperious.

"—doing very well." Kathy ignored the order. Crying openly now, she spilled out, "You're killing us with this situation." Her voice rose but had an undertone of resentment beneath the fear. "Do you realize this?"

Energized by her boldness and anger, Kathy rushed on. "She's on medication, she might not make it. You might take both parents from me!" She stopped as a moan filled her throat.

The caller cut in, his tone ominous. "Listen to me very carefully. You will go and buy white pants, a white T-shirt and a white jacket, and a big, big backpack, or a big book bag. You're to put the money all in that bag."

Again, Mary Ellen drew Kathy's eyes to the script with suggested replies and new ways to control the conversation. Mary Ellen's coaching grounded Kathy, and as such, it helped, but Kathy was essentially on her own. Mary Ellen circled a question they had rehearsed.

Kathy stalled the caller as she tried to formulate her words. "Do—is—is there any way—my mom and I … that we could get, like, a courier to drop this off?" She looked into the distance and bravely tried to swallow a sob. "'Cause I don't know if I can handle this!" She could hear the low thunder of her pulse thudding in her neck and wrist.

"Look, look!" The kidnapper raised his voice. "Do you want to see your dad again? You have to make the drop using your mom's Jaguar. *Listen!*" he bellowed, clearly annoyed by her incessant weeping.

With the caller's reference to the car, Mary Ellen squeezed Kathy's arm and nodded firmly as she tapped a few more lines on the script. Kathy acknowledged with her eyes. All the agents had nixed the Jaguar, and it was her job to steer the kidnappers toward a bigger car, one with ample room to conceal an agent on the floor behind the front seat. She'd been clearly coached on the issue. Now she was on the line to make it happen.

"It's—I have to tell you … I've been trying to—to start the Jaguar and it won't start and … I don't know what's wrong with it. Can I use the Cadillac?"

The kidnapper didn't hesitate. "How about your Honda Civic? I know you have a silver Honda Civic."

Kathy stalled again, panicked, searching. "Can I—" They hadn't covered this possibility. *Think quick!* Suddenly she said, "But I don't have my car. My boyfriend has it." She was gambling that the garage door hadn't been raised since she'd pulled her Honda inside Wednesday morning. If it had, and if they were watching ... it was a chance she had to take.

"Use the blue Cadillac then. Look—don't give me shit!" The caller's exasperation was closer to the surface. "Now cut the bullshit!"

"Okay, okay." As she nodded into the phone, Kathy saw Mary Ellen's thumbs-up sign. She was doing well, but she was close to breaking with the intensity.

"I'll call you tomorrow, around, after five or six o'clock."

Kathy concentrated, frowning at the script. "Are we going to make the drop tomorrow—or ... I mean, I don't know how many more days we can take of this. Can't we do it tonight?" She was begging, her voice straining with emotion.

He replied with force. Mary Ellen was not surprised by his obvious need to take control and dictate the terms of the plan. "Kathy, you're gonna listen to me, and you're gonna do exactly as I say. And I don't want to hear you crying ... "

"Okay, okay," she said meekly, pressing a tissue under her nose. She could back off now. Unbelievably, she had gotten him to agree to using the Cadillac.

"I will call you tomorrow after six o'clock. Have your white pants ready, your white T-shirt and white jacket ready."

"Okay," Kathy was swaying slightly. "Tell my dad we love him," she sobbed.

Mary Ellen directed Kathy's eyes to the script yet again, willing her composure to hold a minute longer.

Kathy read from the paper word for word. "Are you going to release my dad right after I give you the money?"

"We'll ... we'll release him in one hour after—your dad is not even in the state. He is in Mexico. We'll ... "

Kathy pressed. "But you're going to release him after I give you the money, right? Where will you bring him?"

"He'll be in the city—"

"City of what? San Francisco?"

"Yes."

"He's alive, right?" Mary Ellen was amazed and impressed. Kathy was actually firing questions at the kidnapper. Something had energized her.

"Didn't you hear ... ?"

"Okay. Okay."

" ... last time I'm telling you, don't gamble with your dad's life. Now what was the name of that stockbroker you said?"

"What?" Kathy looked at Mary Ellen. They were both surprised. The caller was still off-balance; Kathy had confused him. Excellent. Mary Ellen made rapid notes for turning his sliver of uncertainty into an advantage in the next day's call. "Alex, um ... Brown," said Kathy slowly, puzzled and cautious.

With a reminder that Kathy should be home after six o'clock the next day, the kidnapper hung up. Kathy dropped the receiver and leaned heavily against Mary Ellen, breathing rapidly and shallowly through her mouth.

· EVENING ·

Chuck

Constant fear is a strange bedfellow. If I let myself dwell on thoughts of my family or what these jerks were capable of doing to me and to them, I would begin to shake and swell with nausea. But that wasn't useful to me. Developing a strategy for my release was the only thing that would keep me alert and keep my fear at bay.

Gradually, my bladder stopped clenching when one of the kidnappers—usually Rock—snapped the safety lock of the gun in my ear. I learned to swallow over the knifelike clamp on my gut that sliced through me when they suddenly dropped the elephant chains beside me. Once in a while, when they were talking about Nan or Kathy and the red blindness of rage and terror swam before my dead eyes and pounded like the ocean in my ears, I was able to slow my thudding heart by taking prolonged deep breaths. But not often.

I had to adapt or be killed. It was simple as that. The hard part was knowing what to adapt *to*. Rock was the wild card—the muscle man, the thug. He said little, and when he did speak, I struggled to follow his thinking.

"Do you love your wife?" Rock said suddenly. I sensed the heat of him standing in front of me. He had just come in from working on his weights in the garage, and his words sounded harsh in the abrupt stillness that followed the dropping of dumbbells onto cement and the overloud rock music that blared during his workouts. Steve had left a while ago to make the afternoon phone call, and I had been slumped against the wall, dozing. I sat up, instantly alert to the possible meaning of this odd question coming from Rock.

"What do you mean?" I said warily, trying to swallow rapidly enough to squelch the sharp pain that jolted my intestines.

"What if we take *her*? Set you free and take her?" Rock said. "How much would you give us if we did that?"

I wanted to tell him that if he had Nan, I would give him everything I owned, every penny I could beg or borrow. And then some. Any amount. For Nan or Kathy or Peter or John or my father to be captive in the hands of criminals with guns was unthinkable. In that moment of panic, I was actually grateful that I was the one they had chosen.

Think strategy, Chuck. Money is all that matters to these guys. Make him think the money is all but in his hand, that his current plan is brilliant and his best chance for success. That will divert him from thinking of kidnapping Nan. God, please, don't let them be thinking that. Let them do what they want to me, but please keep Nancy safe.

"You know what my wife and family mean to me," I said, unable to hide the huskiness in my voice. "You know I'd give whatever I had to get them back." *Think strategy.* "But it would be much more complicated. It would probably take weeks to get more money. And there would be more people looking for you. It would be all over the news." I kept going, rambling, making things up, because I had a feeling that Rock was listening to me.

"You have a good plan. It seems to be working. My family is cooperating, and they might even get the money sooner than you asked for. If you stick with your plan, you'll have tons of money. If you try something different, it could take a lot longer and a lot more could go wrong." That was the most I'd talked to either of them since the first day of captivity. Had I overstepped? Would they be suspicious? Would they gag me? It was a risk I had to take if it diverted Rock's attention from Nan.

Rock said nothing. The room was absolutely still for a minute or two. Then he walked past me and clicked on the television. I exhaled loudly. According to the announcer, the early evening news was just ahead and would be followed by another NBA playoff game. Once again, I was grateful for the distraction of the basketball game.

A car door slammed, and the front door opened. Steve had returned. He rustled some paper bags, causing an odor of hot grease to drift through the room. Something landed on my lap: a hamburger, from the shape and weight of it. I was too nervous to eat, hoping he would talk about the phone call. I didn't have long to wait.

"Goddamn it to hell!" Steve sputtered, talking through a mouthful of food. I froze, wondering why he was angry. What had happened? Were they thwarting him? What was going on at home?

"Your daughter. This—Kathy. Says she can't use her mother's Jaguar ... says the Cadillac is—"

I took a chance at interrupting. It might smooth things over, and I hoped and guessed that Kathy was angling to use the safer, more dependable car. "Do you remember I told you yesterday that the Jaguar is not a good car to use for this? It's not driven much. The battery is unreliable, and it doesn't always start. She probably—"

"Doesn't she know how to follow directions? Those were *not* my instructions! Doesn't she know *I'm* in charge? *She* is trying to negotiate with *me* ... and she—"

My heart exploded with pride. I wanted to yell and shout and laugh crazily. *That's my girl. My girl is taking charge for me. Kathy, sweetheart, you're getting us off this island!*

I tried to help her out. "The Cadillac is much more dependable."

"She wants to use your Cadillac—the blue Cadillac Seville. We know all about your cars. But it's too big. Someone could hide in the trunk of that car. I want her to use her Honda Civic. She says her boyfriend has it, so she *has* to use the Cadillac."

"Well, the Honda has very old tires. The Cadillac is safest. Less chance that car trouble would mess up your plan." I tried to sound like I really wanted them to succeed.

Steve grunted and continued to chew noisily. I noticed again how important cars were to Steve and Rock. At some point every day, they talked of models and years and features and colors and speed. It was incredible to think that these punks were ready to kill me to get money to buy cars.

Things were quiet for a time. I ate most of the hamburger and drank a kid-sized carton of milk. They led me to the bathroom, and after that I sat back down on my sleeping bag in the corner of the room. I forced myself to follow the game to distract me from the gnawing worry that Kathy was in exceptional danger right now. I couldn't stand to think that I was the cause of it.

At halftime, someone lowered the volume and Steve started to talk again. "Do you know a man named Mr. Brown?" His question conveyed a hint of challenge, and I tried to be cautious, not understanding.

"I—well, I really can't think of anybody I know named Mr. Brown … except, maybe, a woman at work I know. Her husband would be Mr. Brown, but I can't imagine why you would ask about him."

"You mean you don't know a Mr. Brown?" Steve said sharply. He was clearly agitated. Apparently I had given the wrong answer. I struggled to figure out where this could be leading.

"I don't think so. No."

"Is he some kind of banker?" Steve was standing very close to me now. I could see a fuzzy outline of his pants legs from beneath the blindfold.

"Oh, do you mean Alex Brown?"

"Yeah, that's it—Alex." He walked away from me, rattling the ice in his cup.

So that was it. I exhaled in relief. Steve wouldn't be likely to know that Alex Brown was the name of an investment banking firm on the East Coast. I explained my banking relationship with the company, and Steve seemed okay with it. But he had other suspicions.

"How can they get the money so fast? Is that reasonable? Your daughter said she could have it tonight."

I had no idea how hard or easy it was for Alex Brown to get a huge amount of cash within two days, but something told me I could help by letting Steve and Rock think everything was going according to plan. So I made up an answer.

"Well, uh ... Alex Brown has been in business practically since the Revolution, and ... and they're located in Maryland, which is, ah, you know, close to the Federal Reserve bank, so I suppose they could get cash pretty fast."

Steve grunted. "Yeah, okay, okay."

I couldn't believe he bought my crazy story, but he stopped questioning me.

"Thanks, Lord, for putting the words in my mouth! Stay with me."

I tried to stay alert to their moods. Rock was mostly belligerent, antsy. Since he seemed to be the one who handled the gun most of the time, any movement from him frightened me. There was an undercurrent of violence in his aggressive questions, his taunting me with the gun and the chains. I was terrified I would say or do something that would push him over the edge. I had no doubt that he would kill me in a heartbeat if he was threatened.

Steve was a different story. He seemed to relish being in control and was obviously the mastermind behind the abduction plot—unless there really was a major organization directing them from Lebanon. At the moment, Steve was more interested in impressing me with his TV-fantasy scheme of escape by hauling the ransom money under

Monterey Bay in a one-man submarine.

Were they sane? I didn't think either one was very smart, which made them all the more dangerous. I was constantly afraid I might anger or annoy them, so I kept trying to make them believe their plan was sure to work.

Sitting as quietly as I could in my corner that night, with the drone of the basketball announcer in the background, I realized how much I really *wanted* them to succeed. I wanted them to get every dollar they asked for and then to permanently disappear. If they succeeded, they would be out of our lives forever. My life and my family's lives were dependent on their success. In some convoluted coil of my brain, I began to root for them.

"Have you ever been poor?" It was Steve talking. There was a tension in his words. "Did you always have money for whatever you wanted?"

He seemed to want something from me, some momentous universal answer to life's injustices. I wanted badly to give him the answers he expected, but I was scared I couldn't. Not being sure how Steve's odd mood would impact me, I was cautious.

"Well, maybe not poor, but my parents were working-class people and I didn't grow up with much money."

"I have to have money for my kids," he said, ignoring my reply. "Sometimes they don't even have enough to eat. I need to give them a better life."

I wondered whether Steve was playacting. He sounded sincere, but I thought about the thousands of dollars he said they invested in the so-called "sophisticated" submarine and torpedoes he was so proud of or in renting this house to facilitate a crime. Then the pervasive fear drove away all thoughts other than the will and need to help them succeed in order to save myself.

"If I get free, maybe there's some way I can help your children. Maybe—" Ideas were spinning in my head. This might be the way to save us all!

"I can't afford to send them to college. I want them to go to college," he said, still talking rather softly, as if to himself.

"There are scholarships, there are people I know who ... maybe I could set up a scholarship." I was talking fast and my thoughts seemed disconnected. If they let me go, I would promise to help them and we would all be able to live in peace. If I helped the kidnapper's family, I would help my own. Was it possible we would even be friends one day?

Steve ignored me. Even so, a sliver of hope broke loose. I could feel it colliding with the constant underlying fear that lived in my brain and my belly. Hope was in a desperate battle to win.

FRIDAY | MAY 29

· MORNING ·

Nan

THE FRIDAY MORNING sun did its best to fill the cracks at the edge of the curtained windows, insinuating its warmth and cheer into my bed, into my eyes. I turned in to the pillow, reaching backward for the already dissolving darkness and deadness of sleep. How could we have passed another day and night with no word of Chuck? How much longer could we live like this?

I threw off the covers with a burst of energy fueled by the fear that came rushing in with the return to consciousness after sleep. I charged into the bathroom and groped for the pack of cigarettes I'd left on the back of the toilet. Lighting one, I opened the small door on the back wall and stepped onto the narrow wrought iron balcony that overlooked the backyard.

It was quiet, except for birdsong, and it was beautiful. The dogwood tree was budding, and my roses were beginning to bloom, with promising patches of yellow and pink in the far corner near the brick wall. The grass was unthinkably green. I was struck with the irony that my own backyard, bursting with the color and life and promise of a new season, was betraying me. As it became more vivid, more joyous with each new day of spring, I was slowly being rendered colorless, joyless, and lifeless, withered by loss. I inhaled deeply and held the smoke until it burned in my nostrils.

Despite the sun, my bare feet were cold on the porch floor and my pajamas were scant protection against the morning chill. But I didn't go in. Instead, I leaned my elbows on the railing. With the advantage of height, I spotted one croquet wicket from Monday's game bent under a bush.

For the space of one breath, I was sure that I could call downstairs and tell Chuck he had missed a wicket when he gathered them up Tuesday morning. Sure that I would hear him yell back that he'd grab it on his way to the car. That I would be standing here on my balcony like a guardian angel, watching and loving the top of his graying head as it bobbed below me on his way through the fragrant grass. That we would be starting another ordinary day in our comfortable, ordinary lives. *Oh, Chuck!*

After I dressed, I went downstairs. No one was in the kitchen, though I could hear low voices in the living room. Probably Agent O'Toole and the other female agent who came in and out to give Mary Ellen her occasional breaks. All the male agents had kept very low profiles since Mary Ellen had arrived. I suspected it was part of her job to keep them away from me. I knew they were guarding the house from several vantage points, but discreetly.

I know I freaked them out with my paranoia on Tuesday night. No apologies, though. They gave me every reason to distrust them at that moment. Mary Ellen calms us all. Fine with me if she's the only one we have to deal with right now.

Peter came in just as I finished making coffee. He sank onto the sofa in the den, on the other side of the kitchen counter that divided the two rooms.

He looked over at me. "You doing okay, Mom?" he asked. Concern clouded his eyes, and his face was pale.

"I'm all right. How about you?"

"Throat's still sore, but I'll live." His face went paler as he recognized the unintended mockery of his words. "Crap," he said, looking away from me.

I brushed past his discomfort. "Coffee?" I asked.

"Yeah. Thanks, Mom."

We saved ourselves with the busy little routine of getting cups, pouring coffee, finding milk in the fridge. Peter went outside to get the *Chronicle,* and we traded it off, section by section. Someone— maybe one of the agents—had also put today's *Mercury News* on the counter. I burned the front-page headline into memory: "Voters lost in a barrage of candidate attack ads." Yesterday's headline had proven to us that Chuck was alive. Would he say these words from the *Mercury* today? Would they provide us with hope for at least a few more hours?

With Peter absorbed in the sports pages, I wound my way back upstairs with a cup of coffee. I hoped Kathy would sleep a while longer. None of us needed to talk. There were no longer any words that gave our family conversations meaning. Our anxiety—for Chuck, for our John, for Grandpa Matt, for one another, for ourselves—was so palpable that it felt like a cloak thrown over us, muffling our voices.

I resolved to spend the day in the laundry room, ironing. The tiny room off the upstairs hall was the perfect place to be alone, and the rote, soothing motion of the iron would allow me to think and pray as I worked. I arranged myself and a stack of clothes to face the sunshine that streamed through the small window overlooking the street.

I was only a few steps from the catwalk portion of the stairwell that overlooked the downstairs entry hall. Feeling hidden, but close enough to follow the activity downstairs, I decided to iron every garment in the house if I had to.

About 11:00, the front doorbell rang, not in itself unusual these past few days as several friends and neighbors, apparently realizing they'd not seen or heard from Chuck or me of late, stopped by or called to check on us. Peter was doing a masterful job of redirecting people, begging contagion, laryngitis—whatever worked—to make our unsuspecting callers leave the front porch or hang up the phone as quickly as possible.

This visitor was different. The moment I heard Peter call out, "Kathy, flowers for you," I was startled by a rush of voices and running footsteps. I hurried to the banister and watched, astonished, at the scene unfolding below me.

Three black-jacketed FBI agents had grabbed the flowers from Peter's hand almost before the delivery man had turned to leave the porch. One of the agents, running over from his surveillance post on the street, detained the delivery man outside, while the other two, alerted by radio at their backyard stations, pushed Peter well away and immediately began to dismantle the flowers, stem by stem, petal by petal.

Hearing the commotion, Kathy came from her bedroom down the hall to stand with me at the railing. Never reluctant to get involved, she called down to them, "Hey, wait a minute! Those flowers are for me! What the heck are you doing?" She started downstairs.

"Stay where you are, Kathy," said one of the agents, still pulling at moss and sifting dirt. There was no mistaking the command in the polite request. Kathy halted midstairs.

We all stood watching as though we were behind a police barrier: Peter on the left, at the entrance to the dining room, Mary Ellen on the right toward the living room, Kathy and me looking down from above. In a matter of minutes, the square of floor just inside the front door was littered with bright crushed blooms, straggling ferns, and little piles of dirt and moss. The air was creased with the tart green odor of pinched leaves.

The agent outside the door gave the delivery truck the okay to go. He reached into the mess and extracted a crumpled white card. "Happy Graduation, Kathy," he read. "From the Meindls." He looked up at Kathy and me and smiled an apology. "Sorry, folks," he said, shrugging his shoulders. "Had to be done. Could've been a bomb, a poison, a trick, a message—anything. Doing our job, is all."

Kathy sat down on the steps, exhaling loudly through her mouth. "Yeah, we know," she said.

Still slightly stunned, we stared for a minute at the vivid ruins of intended celebration. Kathy stood and stretched. "I need to call the Meindls and thank them for the gift," she said. She looked over at me with a cautious, awkward grin, which I returned. Slowly, tentatively, we all—agents and family—smiled at one another in an odd camaraderie.

"We can send you another one, ma'am," said one agent as he unraveled the cord from the vacuum Peter brought in.

"No, no, don't worry about it," I said quickly.

We all slipped away quietly—Kathy to the telephone, Peter to his computer, Mary Ellen to her makeshift office in the living room, the outside surveillance team back to duty stations, and me to the sanctuary of the laundry room and the comfort of freshly washed clothes, rising steam, and the heft of an iron.

I felt old and very tired. I longed for my mother to talk to. It had been five years since she had died. She hadn't seen any of her grandchildren graduate from college. She had suffered the death of a daughter—my younger sister Kathy—who died just before Mom. Doesn't death respect anybody, anything? I remembered my grandmother. What had she endured? And me? What more was in store for me? *Death doesn't respect anybody ....*

As my arm developed a regular rhythm of broad strokes on the flat items—I liked to iron uncomplicated things like pillowcases—I began a litany of prayers, naming my family, remembering them, calling on them, loving them. *Mom ... Dad ... Kathy ... Dee-Dee ... Uncle Tom ... Aunt Rose. I know you're all in heaven. Do something! Ask God to do something! Watch over Chuck and protect him. Please. Keep him safe, Mom. And help us get through this—whatever it is.*

By noon I was drowsy with the heat from the sun and the iron meeting over the ironing board in the small room. I was about to take a cigarette break on my little backyard balcony when the doorbell rang again. I heard a male voice telling Peter that the box was okay. Apparently the agents had intercepted the delivery outside and vetted it there.

I peered out the door into the hall. Peter was on his way upstairs with a Talbots box. "Is this your dress for John's graduation, Mom?" He smiled at me, willing me to be enthusiastic, I knew. I saw the sadness in his eyes. We were all thinking the same: Would we all be going to the graduation? Would there be a family vacation afterward on Nantucket Island? I felt a stab of longing for John. My poor son cut off from us, unaware. It felt cruel.

For Peter, I knew a deeper sadness: Would we be a family at his wedding only a few months away? Would his father see his first son take a bride and his first joyful steps toward building a home and family of his own? For Peter's sake, I tried for a modicum of cheer. Kathy suddenly interrupted my thoughts, calling as she and Mary Ellen entered the front hall from the kitchen where they had been prepping for the next phone call, the event that hovered over each hour like the rotten-sweet smell of decay. "Is that your Talbots dress, Mom? Cool. Why don't you try it on for us? I'm dying to see it."

There was a false note in Kathy's enthusiasm. Effort. The last thing I felt like doing was trying on a pretty new dress for an anticipated family event. The dress, the fit, the event itself—they were now completely irrelevant to us.

But I would try. It would distract us when we needed distraction. If we could pretend for a moment that things were normal, that events would proceed as usual, then we would pretend.

"Okay, sure," I said, hoping my voice wasn't as empty as my desire to participate. "Be right back." I took the box from Peter and went to my room to change.

"Come on down to the kitchen when you have it on," Kathy called after me.

I was just stepping into the crisp white cotton when the phone rang.

126

· AFTERNOON ·

Kathy

A T THE SOUND of the phone—its ringer volume set to maximum—Kathy shot up from the table, overturning the wooden chair behind her. The sunny quiet of the kitchen was shattered. Mary Ellen reached out to steady the receiver in its cradle, then righted the chair, while Kathy stood rigid, frozen as the space between the piercing rings. She had an urge to run. Instead, with concentrated effort, she closed her eyes and clung to the edge of the table.

"Deep breath, Kathy, deep breath." Mary Ellen began the mantra. "Let it ring again."

Kathy sat down cautiously on the edge of the chair, blew out an extended exhale, then moved to the counter and picked up the phone at the end of the third ring. On her right, Mary Ellen held tightly to her upper arm, bracing her.

"Hello?" Her voice echoed like tin in her ear.

"Kathy. Is the money ready?" Businesslike. No preface.

"Yes, it is." But, oh, it wasn't. She was lying with all her might. *Tell him you have the money*, Mary Ellen had said earlier. *It will be ready when you need it. Be positive no matter what. Comply. Cooperate. Tell him what he wants to hear.* Kathy was ready to throw psychology out the window. She had to get on with this, get it over with. Get Dad home.

"Now, which car are you—" the caller began.

"Is my dad okay? Can I have another—"

"You will hear, you will listen to—"

"Another tape?" she persisted, ignoring the annoyance in his voice.

"You're going to *listen!*"

Mary Ellen held her hand up, palm flat. The "back off" gesture. Kathy stayed silent.

The kidnapper continued. "Get the morning edition of the *San Jose Mercury News* and keep it with you. We will call you tonight at ten o'clock and give you specific—"

She couldn't help herself. "Oh, can't we do it earlier than that? I, I, my mom—"

"*Listen to me!*"

Something snapped inside her. "Why don't you listen to *me*, okay? My family's a mess. I'm a wreck. It's only me here, and I'm trying to keep my life together. I want to get this over with!"

She saw another "don't push him, don't make him mad" hand signal from Mary Ellen. More urgent this time. Kathy was suddenly fearful. What if he got mad and didn't call back? The caller was their only link to her dad. Mary Ellen preached that sermon every day.

"Look. This will be all over tonight if you do exactly as I say. Again, don't do anything stupid. No games. If you're being followed, the mission will be canceled. If you're—"

"Okay." She followed Mary Ellen's pencil down the page to a question they had rehearsed less than an hour ago. "But how do I know you won't kidnap *me*? That you won't hurt me?"

"We don't want nothing to do with you. All we want is the money."

"As soon as I drop off this money, will I see my dad?" Now her voice felt small and hollow. She hoped she sounded meek if that was what he wanted.

"Your dad will be released in a few hours, I told you."

A jolt of fear raised her voice. "You—no—you said an hour yesterday! You told me one hour." She punched the final words to make her point.

"Two hours at most. He told me last night that after you make the drop, you are to go directly home and wait for his phone call."

"All right." *Be cooperative, Kathy.*

"Now listen very carefully because I got about ten more seconds and I'm gonna have to hang up. If you're being followed—"

"I understand about being followed." She felt like drumming her fingers. Get *on* with it!

"If the money is bugged or there's transmitters or—"

Enough! "Do you think I'm stupid?" She was not successful at keeping the sarcasm from her voice but all the same got a thumbs-up sign from Mary Ellen this time. It was good to repeat language the kidnapper used. That much she had learned two days ago.

He was wrapping it up. " ... and be home tonight at ten o'clock, and you'll get a phone call with further instructions."

He disconnected. Kathy put her head in her hands and shook with a vehemence independent of her will. Mary Ellen kept her arms tight around Kathy's shoulders, but the shaking didn't subside until Peter came up from the ground-floor study and enfolded her in the kind of squashing hug that only brothers can give, murmuring all the while how awesome she was, how smart, how strong. By the time he and Mary Ellen led her into the living room for the routine postcall debriefing, Kathy almost believed him.

• • •

FBI

THE MINUTE they picked up a possible trace on the call, the FBI tech team at the Geschke house called in the location to Special Agent Ken Thompson at the Incident Command Post operating out of the Bureau's San Jose resident agency (RA). Thompson and his communications team broadcast the call information to the fan of field agents on standby in the area and those in the RA—all awaiting orders.

Thompson was frustrated. The only positive lines they could draw were still too broad to suit him: public phone booths in Gilroy and Aromas, in the general area of Hollister. To say the caller was somewhere in southern Santa Clara County or northern Monterey County was hardly narrowing it down.

Their more sophisticated trap-and-trace devices weren't performing well, partly due, he believed, to the small-town phone systems with older, mom-and-pop public phones that dotted the farm belt running south of San Jose. They often couldn't identify a specific street, much less a specific phone.

The drop was set for tonight, and they wouldn't even have a location until after the next call at 10:00 PM. Not enough time to set up the best net. He wanted a complete surround: from land, from sky, and for all they knew in this case, maybe from sea. Agent Thompson didn't like the odds.

As supervisor of the San Jose satellite agency, Thompson had kept his finger on the pulse of the Geschke abduction case since the first call from Adobe's John Warnock on Tuesday evening. Along with his boss and special agent in charge of the San Francisco office, Dick Held, Thompson and his team were responsible for the mobilization effort that would cover the drop and, best case, rescue the victim and make the arrest.

The operation was huge. More than two hundred agents were on alert. One hundred agents had been rapidly dispersed throughout the Bay Area on Tuesday night as standard protocol. SWAT teams, sniper teams, evidence recovery teams (ERTs), and surveillance operations groups (SOGs) were all on standby.

Helicopters had been requisitioned from the military base at Fort Ord, just south of Monterey, and were ready for takeoff. Area maps dotted with pins showing current agent positions covered the walls of the tactical command post. Every team, every agent, had a specific job, and the communications team constantly funneled information one to the other. They were prepped and geared, ready to jump—but couldn't. They lacked one critical piece of information: location.

Despite the aggravation of waiting, Agents Thompson and Taylor rarely felt this sharp, this alive, though they'd had precious little sleep since Tuesday night. The command center hummed with intensity, the men and women in it driven by the single desire that gave meaning to their training and their careers: to save a life and protect an innocent family.

Thompson surveyed his maps again and listened to the buzz around him. Waiting. He set his mouth in a grim line, remembering the debate yesterday with his boss, Dick Held. Thompson was against using the daughter for the drop. "We're putting an innocent civilian in harm's way," he had argued.

"To make it work, we have to go with the evidence," Held had countered.

In every phone call so far, the kidnapper had shown that he knew details about the Geschke family. He had researched them. It was likely he knew Kathy Geschke's voice and face and build. If they used an agent stand-in, they could scare him off and lose their only connection to the victim. Held had put it something like this: "The guy IDs her as an agent, we lose the trail to Chuck."

Thompson conceded to the logic, but he still didn't like it. He thought of the unknowns: a possible trapped criminal with a gun, the incredible danger for a person without training. He thought about Kathy Geschke, and then of his own little girl, not all that much younger. Damn it! You couldn't put a bulletproof vest on your head.

The afternoon crawled toward evening. At regular intervals,

Thompson and his team reviewed the systems in place. Area weather reports showed a late fog moving in south of San Jose in the region of the phone calls, but it wasn't too worrisome, especially since they didn't have any idea of where they were headed to follow the drop. Could be north, which was bright and clear.

The money situation *was* worrisome. By the late afternoon report, hundreds of bills still had to be photocopied and marked in San Francisco. Then they'd have to be bundled and wrapped with an invisible transmitter to allow for the trace.

The marked money and a backup transmitter would be flown to the San Jose agency to be repacked in the type of black bag specified by the kidnapper. A duffel bag would be best. After a final beeper check, the carefully prepared bag would be delivered to the Geschke home in Los Altos and placed in the passenger seat beside Kathy Geschke in the wired Cadillac.

The money had been raised quickly from the sale of family stock and investments. It was then transferred to the Federal Reserve Bank of San Francisco, where the evidence team had been working since Wednesday. Now they were down to the wire and getting heat from the field.

Thompson understood the pressure. Counting, copying, and invisibly marking $650,000 in $100 bills was a daunting task. It meant handling 6,500 individual bills, each more than once. Thompson doubted the family—or anybody outside the Bureau or a bank—could understand the time it would take.

Things in Los Altos were moving faster. Agent O'Toole's recent update had confirmed that the Cadillac was with the tech team and that the monitors had been installed. They were running tests now. Dick Held had designated Harry Fujita to be Kathy Geschke's bodyguard and protector, concealed only inches from her on the floor of the car behind the driver's seat. That comforted Ken Thompson a little about sending the young woman into the danger zone.

Fujita was a rock: strong, solid, and intimidating. He was also more expert than anyone Thompson knew with the Remington 870 shotgun he'd be carrying. If he sensed Kathy was in danger, the short-barreled, wide-range weapon would allow Agent Fujita to pop up from hiding and instantly spray up to nine pellets in one round to take out anyone within twenty-five yards of the car. Harry knew the weapon, knew the peril, knew the procedure. If Kathy had to do this dangerous job, Fujita was the best protection she could have.

Thompson's radio interrupted his thoughts. San Francisco calling: The money was ready. It would be in San Jose by seven o'clock. Progress.

· EVENING ·

Kathy

THEY WERE SO SLOW, the FBI. So irritatingly careful—and slow. Slow to bug the car, slow to mark the money. They had promised it as early as yesterday afternoon, but here it was past seven o'clock on Friday night, and it *still* wasn't here. What if the kidnapper called early? What if he wanted her to leave *now?*

Kathy walked across the empty kitchen to the fridge to get a Coke. As her fingers gripped the icy can, she thought briefly that hot tea would be a better choice to rout the chill that rose from the hollow of her stomach at the thought of talking to this revolting man again. She and Mary Ellen were meeting at eight o'clock to role-play.

This phone call was it: the location of the drop. Their best and only chance to get this crazy jerk to lead them to her dad. The final contact. *Please don't let him drag this out any longer, Lord. I can't, we can't, take it anymore. And Dad. How can he stand it?*

Kathy stopped at the sink where the window overlooked the front yard and street and stared into the gathering dusk. In her mind she saw again, distinctly, the brooding face of the olive-skinned, black-haired man who had driven by the house yesterday as she was walking to the front gate to pick up the mail. She remembered how he had deliberately slowed and stared at her. How she had refused to turn away. *I know it was him. He's watching us. He's blackmailing us. He has Dad.*

Voices drifted in from the living room. The Warnocks had come an hour ago with food—John, Marva, and their son Chris, whom the FBI had interviewed along with his parents on Tuesday. The three of them had hauled in the plates of wrapped sandwiches and covered containers of salad that were now spread across the table. They put bowls of pretzels and chips and nuts on countertops and lamp tables. As if they had come to some kind of vigil. Did they think it was a wake? She took a long pull on her Coke and relished the burn that snaked down her throat and dropped to her stomach. The usually sweet aftertaste was bitter.

It was lucky for Mom to have close friends with her. As for Pete, he must be aching to talk to Diane. And what was Diane going through? She couldn't imagine the questions Diane must have and the trust it would take to believe your fiancé was so sick he went to his parents' house and you couldn't see him for days. *Hang in with us, Diane. By tomorrow, you'll know. You'll understand.*

Pete obviously liked having Chris Warnock around. He could unload to Chris about the tough things and then kid around in that guy-to-guy way that lifted everybody's spirits. So, good for Pete.

For her part, she wanted to be alone. She didn't want to pray anymore. She didn't want to think anymore. Or rehearse anything. Or walk on eggshells because she might enrage a crazy, greedy, dangerous, disgusting, insane creature to do some crazy, dangerous deed. She just wanted to get her directions, dress in the cheap white clothes the kidnapper ordered, pack the money, and *go!* An hour or two after that, Dad would call them. Safe. Free. Then she would sleep for a long, long time.

The kitchen lights came on, and Kathy saw a distorted version of herself in the window glass. She quickly turned around. Mary Ellen had come into the kitchen and switched on the overhead lights near the door.

"Agent Fujita just got here from San Jose with the money," she said. "He's already packed the Eddie Bauer bag and stowed it in the Cadillac."

Kathy nodded, not trusting her voice. The anger and bravado of a few minutes ago had suddenly deserted her. This unspeakable event was really going to happen.

"Are you ready to go over this once more, Kathy?" Mary Ellen asked gently. "It's nearly eight. I'd like us to talk about a couple of things. Then I'll help you dress for the drive."

"Yes, sure," Kathy said, struggling to emulate Mary Ellen's professional calm. "Want a Coke?" She opened the fridge and grabbed another Coke without waiting for an answer. Kathy liked that Mary Ellen didn't coddle her, never sugarcoated or hid the fact that this was serious and dangerous business.

At times, especially during the phone calls, Kathy felt a fiery, steely force passing from Mary Ellen to herself. She sensed an unremitting toughness wrapped inside the quiet feminine package that was Special Agent Mary Ellen O'Toole. The FBI was full of surprises.

By nine o'clock Kathy was dressed in the white sweats and white T-shirt one of the female agents had purchased yesterday at Sears. The fit was okay, although the cheap pants were boxy and loose. She tightened the drawstring and rolled the waistband to take up some of the slack. They were waiting for her downstairs with the white jacket and black nylon duffel bag packed with thousands of bills.

When Kathy entered the living room, Peter, Chris, and Marva were sitting by the window bay facing the backyard, playing a lackluster game of cards. Mom was back upstairs reading, Pete told her. *All of us bracing ourselves against the dreaded ring of the phone,* she thought. Mary Ellen called to her from the kitchen, and she turned away from the appealing comfort of the scene in the living room. It was time for the final prep.

· · ·

He called at 9:28 pm. "Are you ready?" he barked. "Listen very carefully..."

Within seconds, after the loud click of the tape recorder, her father's dull, distant voice was on the line, twisting into the kitchen. "Hi, Nancy. Hi, Kathy. This is Chuck."

"Oh, God," Kathy moaned.

To prove he was still alive, Chuck read a headline from the *San Jose Mercury News*, which, to their relief, matched with the Friday morning edition lying before them on the kitchen table.

Chuck's recorded voice continued. "Kathy, I remember often saying that if I was stuck on a desert island, you're the one I would depend on to pull me through." At the familiar words of the longtime, half-teasing family story, Kathy began to cry silently, nodding as tears coursed down her cheeks.

"I had no idea it would come to this, and I trust you with my life." Chuck's uninflected words went on. "I ask you not to gamble with your life or Nancy's or mine. Make sure that no one accompanies you in the car ... make sure there are no electronic devices on you or on the money or on the car. I love you both very much." The tape stopped abruptly.

Kathy jumped in and tried to bargain for an immediate release for her father. The caller shouted over her. "*Listen* to me, goddamn it! I'm only gonna say this once, and I'm gonna hang up. Do you have a paper and pen ready?"

Desperate to get every syllable, she pushed the receiver painfully tight against her ear. The directions were very specific: Take the 280 South to 101 South to 156 West. Then take Route 1 South to the Reservation Road exit. Go right on Reservation Road and then an immediate right on Dunes Road.

"Okay, okay. That's a right, then another right?" Anxiety pinched her voice in her throat. The three agents in the room with her were scribbling the routes along with her. Harry Fujita had already rushed past her toward the back of the house, pulling out his radio as he ran.

Kathy squeezed her eyes shut to better focus on the voice in her ear: " ... a right turn on Reservation Road, then another immediate right on Dunes Road. You go all the way to the end of the street until you can't go any farther and you drop the money."

"Okay." She couldn't keep her breathing steady. She was gulping air.

"You keep on going. You make a U-turn and go back the same way you came. If there is anybody with you, they will be shot."

Kathy retreated to the safety of a stock phrase. "I fully intend to comply with—hello? Hello?" A series of electronic ticks pulsed through the receiver. Some garbled words. "Hello? Hello?" she shouted over the jumble of noise in her ear.

"Yes. Now listen." The noise faded and the caller's words cleared, as though they had pushed through a dense fog.

"Yeah, okay." Thank God she hadn't lost him. She closed her eyes and released the breath she'd been holding. He was probably just fumbling with the tape recorder and caused the static.

"Right now it's 9:30. By 11:30 or before you're gonna be there."

"How long does it take me to—"

" ... exactly an hour and a half, driving at sixty-five. Don't drive any faster than sixty-five. You drive faster, you're gonna get pulled."

"Don't drive too fast," she echoed. Mary Ellen pushed a note toward her. Kathy nodded back and asked, "But how do I know you're not going to kill my dad when I give you the money?"

"Because your dad has not seen our faces. He doesn't know who we are. We don't have nothing to do with him. Now get going!"

The minute Kathy replaced the receiver, an agent began dialing the FBI command post in San Jose where dozens of agents were on stand-by. Mary Ellen nudged her shoulder toward the living room where two more agents were waiting to prepare her for the drive. One of them put a tiny device in her ear and wound the cord under her arm and down her back where he attached it to a small box affixed to her waistband and carefully camouflaged under her shirt.

Pete and the Warnocks circled around her to watch. The other agent handed her an ugly, heavy vest. She made a face at Mary Ellen, who nodded, her mouth tight, and said, "Kevlar, Kathy. It's bullet-proof. You have to wear it." Kathy heard a little gasp from Marva.

One of the men held it up while she backed into him, arms stretched out, awkwardly shrugging into the tight vest. Reddening a little, the agent helped her fasten the grips across her chest and down to her waist. Then he handed her the lightweight nylon jacket which neatly concealed the dark vest and trailing wires.

Kathy tried to bend at the waist but couldn't. She felt poured into the inflexible tube of the vest, her body so rigid she could topple off center at any moment. Worse than being uncomfortable, she felt completely vulnerable, Kevlar or not.

"I can't even bend," she said, wincing as the ribs of the vest cut into her waist.

"Let's try this," said Mary Ellen, reaching into one of the plastic shopping bags scattered on the living room chairs. She pulled out a small box of maxi pads and shoved several of the puffy sanitary napkins under the vest to cushion the pressure at Kathy's waist. *Any other time this remedy would be either ridiculous or hilarious,* Kathy thought. Tonight no one smiled.

The little knot of people watched her cautiously. She imagined them wondering: Should they be solemn, given the chilling circum-stances? Or should they tease her, to distract her and lighten things up? She suddenly wanted to hug them all for being in this outrageous situation with her: Pete and Mary Ellen, Marva, John, and Chris, the agents she recognized and those she didn't and—Mom?

Nan had come downstairs silently. She was standing on the pe-riphery of the little circle in the living room, her eyes locked on Kathy. Kathy instinctively moved toward her but didn't speak. Her mother's face was eloquent enough. In Nan's eyes Kathy saw the helpless fusion of love, terror, grief, pain, and pride. Overcome, they clung to each other for only a moment until Kathy said firmly, addressing everyone and no one, "I have to go. I can't be late."

Mary Ellen moved to the door. "The car's ready, Kathy. Agent Fujita's in place." The circle tightened around her, hugging, blessing, crying.

Kathy was suddenly struck with an urgency so powerful that she propelled herself through the doorway and into the garage, almost running.

"May the force be with you," said Chris Warnock softly as she passed him, breaking into the tension just enough to make them all smile. Even she did, for a split second.

She reached back to touch her mother once more, then stepped into the car, punched the garage door opener, and turned the key. As the overhead door lifted behind her, she looked toward the band of people clustered by the door to the house.

They seemed far away. She was dislocated, hovering above them somehow. Their bodies swam and shifted in her vision like some kind of angels smiling at her through the cloud of exhaust from the motor. It was surreal. A dream. This was not happening. She quickly backed away, down the driveway.

• • •

FBI

SPECIAL AGENT Ken Thompson began shouting out the drop location and the drive route before his phone hit the desk. "Here we go, team! Monterey Beach. Reservation Road exit off Route 1 South. That's Marina."

The San Jose command post, jammed with restless FBI agents, erupted. Senior SWAT Team Leader Tom LaFreniere turned from the wall map, ready to assign his men to the field. Half his team—one ten-man assault team plus two sniper observer teams of two men each—was deployed immediately to Monterey Beach at Marina to survey the drop site and set up surveillance.

LaFreniere put Agents Robinson and Bezick on Dunes Road, closest to the drop. The rest of the attachment would cover the highway at Reservation Road and the dunes on the ocean side. LaFreniere would follow with the remaining sniper and assault units to establish a tight perimeter around the site. Using Robinson's broadcasts of the drop site action, all team positions would be ready to move in any direction as the operation developed.

The current strategy for all teams was to observe and follow whoever picked up the money, delaying questioning or arrest until the subject had led the agents back to the victim. The first SWAT team contingent was on the road for the one-hour drive to Marina within ten minutes after the kidnapper gave Kathy Geschke directions to the drop location. The second group wasn't far behind.

Agents assigned to the special operations groups, Larry Taylor among them, would be stationed on the highway and around the perimeter, monitoring every possible exit point from the beach to the highway for at least a mile surrounding the drop site. They would move in and assist with pursuit depending on radio communication and orders from the tactical operations site commander in the field.

Other units would be setting up an emergency tactical command post close to the site at the Marina police department—a last-minute decision by the special agent in charge, Dick Held, who left San Jose for Marina by helicopter at approximately 10:00 PM. Agent Thompson stayed behind in San Jose to run the communications desk while the command post was in transit. Some of the radio transmitters were failing. Whether it was fog or bad equipment, he didn't know, but Thompson was concerned.

Constant communication with the field was critical to the operation. In the midnight dark, complicated this night by cloud cover and fog, a successful pursuit could be entirely dependent on voice communication to and from the SWATs in the dunes and the surveillance teams on the highway.

Working on the premise that the drop site would be monitored by the criminals and that any suspected police activity could result in injury or death to the victim, the agents had to move in and take up positions unobserved. With nearly forty armed men converging on Monterey Beach, concealment would be tricky. On this score at least, the black sky and thick fog were fortunate.

• • •

Kathy

THE DASHBOARD CLOCK rolled from 10:08 to 10:09 as Kathy drove down University Avenue to El Camino Drive. Her pulse pounded in her ears at the sight of it, and she accelerated involuntarily. The kidnapper had called at 9:30, the call had lasted less than five minutes, and he expected her to leave immediately afterward. He'd calculated the drive time at ninety minutes, so he assumed she would be at the drop site by 11:15. She would be almost thirty minutes late! *He has to wait. He can't leave. Lord, he can't leave. Do you hear me?*

She heard Agent Fujita check in with the undercover FBI surveillance team that surrounded her, though she couldn't say where. Even with police on all sides, she didn't feel safe. The FBI couldn't protect her from the fear in her soul or the trembling in her body.

Kathy merged onto I-280 from El Camino, immediately taking the powerful car past eighty miles an hour. Harry Fujita's calm voice rose up from behind her. "Hey, take it easy, Kathy. He'll wait for you. Remember, you've got the money."

"Yeah. Okay. Okay." She eased back on the accelerator a little, staying in the far left lane. Most of the traffic was in the lanes opposite, going north. Kathy envied them. Probably people her own age heading home after meeting friends for dinner. Maybe moms or dads who worked late, looking forward to a glass of wine and the 11:00 news. How ordinary and dull—and wonderful—it seemed. No one driving with her on the same road would have guessed the drama unfolding in the dark blue Cadillac speeding by them.

Despite the constant static hum of Harry Fujita's walkie-talkie and the terse phrases he exchanged with the unmarked escort cars on the highway, there was an isolating silence inside the car. She wished Agent Fujita would sneeze or breathe or shift his position between the bursts of dialogue on the radios.

"Harry?" Kathy said softly into the dark.

"I'm here." His voice was relaxed.

"You sleepy?"

"Not on your life. Won't happen," he said amiably.

"You're so—so quiet," she said.

"Don't forget I do this for a living," he said. She could hear the smile in his words. "I'm an expert at patience. Sometimes hours and hours without moving."

"Yeah, I guess. Harry?"

"What?"

"I'm glad you're with me."

"Me too, Kathy, me too," he said. "Not a thing going to happen to you if I'm here. Believe me." There was not a whisper of doubt in his tone.

"I believe you." Just words, she knew, but they had a powerfully comforting effect coming from the agile, well-muscled frame of a highly trained government agent with a shotgun.

"The 101 coming up on the right," said a disembodied voice from the radio on the backseat floor with Harry. "Move her over."

"You hear that, Kathy?" asked Fujita.

"Yeah. I saw the sign."

With the lights of San Jose fading on her left, she faced the looming profile of the mountains straight ahead. She moved into the right lane, where the overhead sign indicated the upcoming exit toward Los Angeles on 101 South. Just as she'd been told.

"Do whatever they tell you. These people are serious." Her father's recorded words had never left her mind. *Okay, Dad. This better be the right road to you, 'cause I'm coming fast.*

The merge lane onto 101 was long, curved, and elevated. The line of dark hills, now on her left, created a menacing boundary on the driver's side of the car. She felt simultaneously blocked in and free as she raced along the high ramp, hilltops at her shoulder. The brief, illogical geography gave her a floating sensation. Trapped in the bowl of a valley, yet suspended above it—as if she were watching herself navigate through this improbable, impossible predicament.

Traffic was light as she left the ramp and cut across the highway to the left lane. The stretch down 101 was the longest leg of the trip. She was hot, sweating under the bulky protective vest overlaid with the slippery white jacket that trapped the heat inside. But there was no time to shrug out of the nylon windbreaker to get relief. What relief was there? An exit alert for Bernal Road flashed by on her right, leading traffic through the heart of the Valley.

Silicon Valley. She wished she'd never heard of it. Why had her parents left Pittsburgh all those years ago? She could understand the lure of adventure and opportunity when you're in your twenties. Fair enough. She was in her twenties and was feeling the same pull, so she could forgive them that.

But Dad didn't *have* to leave Xerox. Didn't *have* to start a company. They had a great life before Adobe, before all the money. And now look at them! It was Dad's own fault they were in this predicament! He was chasing his dreams and hauling everyone else along behind. And it had led to this. Maybe to death.

She slapped her fist against the wheel, wishing with all her heart she could yell at her father, argue with him, hurl every computer in their house against a wall. "Stupid, stupid," she whispered fiercely, hating herself and her anger. She wiped her wet face with the back of her hand and groped on the console for a tissue. She blew her nose.

"You all right, Kathy? Don't go losing it now. We need you, every inch of you and then some. We know how tough you are ... stretch it out a little more for us, can you?" Harry sounded more like coach than bodyguard.

"Yeah. I can ... I mean—I guess I can. Okay." Kathy pulled in large mouthfuls of the car's recirculated air, filling her lungs and cheeks, and concentrated on releasing it puff by puff.

"Gilroy's coming up," she said over her shoulder to Harry, as they whizzed past a sign. Her voice and breath were tight but contained.

"Doing good, Kathy," he said. "We're almost halfway."

The Gilroy exit sign was well behind them before Kathy noticed the flat openness of the land around her. The hills that had bordered the road for so many miles had gradually rolled off to the right toward the ocean. The landscape that earlier enclosed her now propelled her into wide, clear, open fields, leaving her more visible and more vulnerable than ever. She suddenly missed the hovering protection of the dark hills.

What was protection? Harry Fujita's gun? Black Kevlar? Was that all? Well, there was no protection from her family. *She* was the one who had to talk to these creeps on the phone. *She* was the one flying through the night trying to save everybody *else*. Dad obviously couldn't protect anyone at the moment; Mom and Pete were safe in the house, being protected; John was thousands of miles away and oblivious. No help there.

So who voted for her to be here? She didn't want to be responsible for this: for Dad's life, for her life, for the future of her whole damn family! Was she so bossy and outspoken that people figured she could handle stuff like this? *Well, I can't! Take this cross off my shoulders, God—please. I just pretend to be strong. Everybody's fooled.*

"Oh, God," she said. "There's the sign for 156." Her hand went to her mouth and the edges of her breathing started to fray. "We're almost there, Harry. Harry, I'm not sure I can do this!"

"Steady, Kathy. It's not our exit yet. We want 156 West, not East. Get a grip, now." Harry's words were mild and sympathetic, but Kathy detected a low thrum of urgency.

The 156 East exit led inland to Hollister, a place she'd never been and never wanted to go. In fact, she'd never drive south on 101 again. *Maybe you won't have to worry about making that choice.* "Shut up," she muttered to the voice in her head.

She focused on the windshield and tried to relax her grip on the wheel. According to the sign, the Hollister exit also led travelers to San Juan Bautista, an old Spanish mission.

One of her schoolbooks from years ago—elementary school, for sure—had a chapter on the California missions. She didn't remember San Juan Bautista. St. John the Baptist. Oh, yeah. Some of religion class filtered back. John the Baptist, "Voice in the Wilderness," "prepare ye the way," and all that. The advance man for Jesus.

Well, if you're out there, St. John, buddy, announce me. Tell 'em I'm coming to save the world—or at least one family. Yeah, right. Or get my head lopped off trying. Hey, St. John, were you afraid because you had to go first? You didn't know if people were going to believe you, ignore you, or kill you. I can relate.

She thought she might laugh out loud any minute. Fill the car with a who-cares-screw-you laugh that would echo through the hills and freeze criminals with fear. But the sound that came out was mangled, a groaning hiccup.

Just then, without warning, the road was wrapped in a lush, dark tunnel of trees. Except for the dense, leafy limbs that bordered the road, she saw nothing in the beam of her headlights but a stretch of black asphalt. After the miles of open fields since they passed Gilroy, she felt caged by the high wall and ceiling of trees. She cracked the window, wanting to inhale the comforting musky smell of turned soil. But another fragrance—fresh, clean, and herbal—sifted in.

"Eucalyptus," said Harry, the word drifting in the dark space between them.

"Oh, a eucalyptus grove, then," she confirmed to herself, and the trees lost all menace. Eucalyptus. The oil they used in salons and spas for relaxation. For healing. She filled her lungs.

As suddenly as they were pulled into the grove, they were ejected out. It couldn't have been more than half a mile long. Her life these last few days had been as dramatic as the abrupt shift in the landscape: from cheerfully planning celebrations—a graduation, a vacation, a wedding—to the terrifying terrain of crime, violence, fear, death.

The landscape inside her head had shifted, too. No longer just student or friend or daughter. She was navigating as an adult with the unbearable burden and power to either save or destroy what she loved most. To alter the course of life for her entire family. She fought down a bubble of nausea.

As she pulled farther away from the channel of eucalyptus, the road began its slow descent to the ocean. Ten minutes to eleven. On a flat stretch, Kathy opened up the heavy car to eighty-five, then ninety, reaching up periodically to wipe away the spontaneous tears that blurred her vision. Maybe she would be on time after all. The kidnapper would be waiting, would let her leave safely, would release her dad that very hour, and by the time she got home, he would be calling them to pick him up. Yes! That's how it would happen.

For a moment, she imagined her white clothes glowing around her like an aura. She was a shimmering white knight galloping to the rescue—no, an angel in black Kevlar flying to free the prisoner. She was redeemer, and the thoughts of certain redemption for her dad rolled faster and faster through her head. Her speed increased to match them. The effect was exhilarating!

The radio sputtered, pulling her back to the reality of the dark night and the speeding car. "Already told her." Agent Fujita was responding to what she guessed was a complaint about her speed. She didn't slow down, but the exhilaration deserted her.

"Kathy, you can't afford to be stopped for speeding. Just drop it down a little," Fujita said.

"Okay, a little," she said, not very contrite. She wasn't worried. Who the hell was going to stop her tonight? Harry had already told her the California Highway Patrol was aware of their route and their mission. So were the Monterey and Marina police. According to Harry, they'd all been told to expect high-speed vehicles on the road and possible activity in the air.

"Should be less than five minutes to the exit for 156 West, Kathy," said Harry's muffled voice from the floorboards. "Be ready."

Her shoulders sagged, and the heavy vest dug into the tops of her thighs. Her hands felt limp on the wheel. The momentary jubilation and sudden certainty of her power to rescue her father from danger and her family from fear had tricked her and drained her energy. The bubble of nausea that still sat at the base of her throat threatened once more to burst.

Worse, terror and dread began creeping out of the corners of her mind, threatening her concentration. Route 156 West was one mile ahead.

• • •

FBI

AGENT TOM LAFRENIERE instructed his sniper observers to move in by foot, putting Agents Robinson and Bezick on the ground about three-quarters of a mile north of the drop site with orders to work inland toward the ocean and south toward Dunes Road. It was after 11:00 when the two left the highway. They had less than half an hour to find an observation post. With one set of high-powered night vision goggles to spot the terrain, one radio and one MP-5 automatic rifle, plus one handgun each, Robinson and Bezick crossed shadowy fields and crept low through the pebbly, dry vegetation leading up to the dunes.

Having to minimize movement and noise over the rough, unfamiliar ground made the hike tedious. It was almost 11:40 PM when the two men selected and moved toward a position just below a ridge, about three hundred yards from the dead-end turnaround specified by the kidnapper. They radioed their position to their assault team, hunkered down somewhere beyond them on Reservation Road. The assault team confirmed that the other sniper observer team was well situated in the dunes across from them, ready to pursue if the subject exited on the ocean side. The ransom vehicle was due on the freeway exit ramp within minutes.

LaFreniere and the second SWAT team had taken up position on Del Monte Road, the northern boundary of their perimeter. Though LaFreniere was less than a mile north, radio communication with his men on the beach and Dunes Road was spotty. It went down completely at intervals. Transmission from the field back to Agent Thompson in San Jose was working—feebly. But Ken Thompson couldn't connect with his boss and operation commander, SAC Dick Held, who was trapped in a helicopter over Marina, unable to land because of fog.

Was there a worse time for senior command to be off-radio? Was there much advantage in moving the tactical operations center when the operation was about to go down? Thompson swore his frustration through clenched teeth and kept trying to raise a signal to Held.

On Dunes Road, however, the sniper team reported a perfect view of the street below them, despite the fog. The night goggles not only magnified the distance, but also amplified the ambient light from the street lamp, giving them almost a daylight view of the cul-de-sac. Motionless, they waited.

• • •

Kathy

THERE WAS NO MOON. Fog licked at the headlights in sudden elongated tongues, narrowing the road to the width of the car. Just as suddenly it would evaporate, leaving only blackness beyond the short yellow path of the car's fog lights. She listened to the frequent weather reports barked through Harry's radio. The fog was steadily rolling in, they said, and thickening. It was zero visibility near the beach, and they couldn't get clearance for the helicopters. Nothing was allowed in the air.

The sign materialized like a vision through shifting layers of mist: EXIT #335, RT. 156-W, MONTEREY PENINSULA. Kathy slowed briefly to merge onto the two-lane road that wound through a small commercial strip and opened on to a semirural, residential stretch. Neat, small houses were set back from the road nestled in trees and shrubs.

Occasionally, a window filtered weak, yellow light through the fog. Once again, Kathy imagined husbands and wives, mothers and fathers in bathrobes and sweats watching late-night TV. Once again, she shuddered, realizing the vast distance between normal life and her present reality. Her legs shook on the brake pedal as she slowed to enter the little town of Castroville, where 156 West became Route 1 South.

Harry spoke. "You're doing great, Kathy. We need you to hang on with us. You've been a rock so far. Hang on, Kathy." His voice was low and firm. Coaching.

"How far now?" she managed to say, pushing the heel of her right hand into one eye to stem the shaking and fresh tears. *I'm trying, Harry. I'm trying, Dad. I'm scared, God, I'm so scared. God help me.*

"About seven miles down Route 1 to our exit. About three minutes the way you drive." Kathy heard the tease in Harry's voice, but she couldn't respond, couldn't even smile. It had been the same with Chris Warnock's *Star Wars* remark when she left the house tonight.

Was that only a little more than an hour ago? Impossible. More like a lifetime ago. She hoped Harry and Chris would both somehow know she appreciated them and understood what they were trying to do. *So many people are trying to help us, but nothing changes. I'm still here in this car and still so scared I could vomit any minute.*

She forced her concentration outward. Castroville was a plucky town, she decided, as she kept swallowing down her nausea. Who else would name its most visible restaurant "The Giant Artichoke" and have the guts to blaze it across the highway into the black of night with giant neon?

A memory nibbled and she tried to grab it—anything to fill the few minutes left before her brain would refuse to be distracted. Dad. Dad and The Giant Artichoke. What was it? They had all eaten there years ago—that was it! On the way back from some family trip, Dad had made a big deal of stopping at the most famous restaurant for miles. They had to experience French-fried artichoke, he said.

She must have been eight or nine years old, and she clearly remembered turning up her nose and pretending to gag at the delicacy her dad insisted she try. Dad laughing, teasing as she tried to choke it down. She didn't make any effort to stem the tears this time.

"Two miles, Kathy. Be strong," Harry said from the floor, his voice and breath the only solid presence in the surreal scene that surrounded her as she drove south from Castroville to Marina: artichoke fields; miles and miles of desolate, open flat land; new green plants pressed to the dirt by a mammoth body of fog, its ragged white tails crisscrossing the car. No houses, no lights, no traffic. She cracked the window and smelled the salt of the ocean, expecting to hear the surf in a matter of minutes.

A distant, raggedy bundle of buildings, cylinders, and shafts poked through a swath of clear space in the dunes. "We're passing some kind of factory on the right," she told Harry. "Is that important?"

As if they heard her, the escort team radioed in to Harry with Kathy's answer. "Cement plant on your right. Sand and gravel operation. Means we're in Marina."

"Reservation Road one mile ahead, Kathy," Harry said, repeating the radioed message.

She moved to the right lane, sobbing now, drawing ragged breaths through her mouth. *What am I doing here? Is this the end of my life?*

Kathy made a rolling stop at the end of the ramp and swung onto Reservation Road. A bold arrow pointed straight ahead to Marina State Beach. *Okay, God. For some reason, you put me here and I want you to know I can do this. So I'm doing it*—now. She wrenched the wheel and accelerated into a hard right turn just before the beach sign. She was on Dunes Road.

It was less than half a mile to the cul-de-sac the kidnapper had described at the end of Dunes Road, but the narrow strip was dark and deserted this close to midnight, except for anemic light from a few low-rate motels sprinkled near the dunes. She crossed a water-filled ravine. Then there was nothing but the slotted dunes fencing on her left, a couple more motels on the right. Kathy opened the window an inch and heard the surf pounding on the other side of the dunes. She wondered if he was hiding out there in the spiny shrubs and fog. Suddenly, she felt a chill and closed the window.

She entered the cul-de-sac on the left side, swinging around the arc to the street lamp just beyond the top of the semicircular drive. Her headlights pierced the low-lying clouds of mist to show scruffy beach vegetation poking through the pebbly sand near the road. "Here I go, Harry," she breathed.

"Remember, don't get out of the car," he said in such an urgent low whisper it came out in a hiss.

Kathy pushed the transmission into park, yanked the Eddie Bauer bag from the passenger seat with a grunt against its weight, opened the door just wide enough to funnel the bag through, and gave it a mighty heave from her lap onto the street below the lamppost. *Free! Wherever you are, you're free now, Dad!*

With one hand on the door handle and the other flying from the gear shift to the wheel, she lurched into drive and spun around the right side of the arc. She hunched low behind the wheel, fully expecting a shot to come crashing through the windshield at any moment. Awkwardly pulling the door closed, she raced by the huddled rows of campers and trailers in the Marina Dunes RV park that rolled back from the cul-de-sac on her left.

"It's done, it's done, it's done," she chanted, fueled by adrenaline, hardly aware she was speaking out loud. "It's over, it's over, we have Dad. We'll get Dad back now, Harry, won't we? We'll get him, Harry. Harry?"

"We'll get him back, honey."

"Right away. An hour. They said an hour. Oh my God."

As Kathy sped onto Route 1 going north, she began to feel the hammering of her heartbeat in her temples, thudding in her ears. And the wetness. Her underarms were soaked, and she could feel the moisture weeping down her back to settle at her waist. Her hands were clammy and began to slip on the wheel. Slowly, she dragged first her right hand, then her left, across the top of her thighs to dry them. Gradually, the pounding lessened.

After ten miles or so, Harry climbed into the passenger seat beside her, unfolding his cramped body with obvious relief. "You did great, Kathy, great," he said. She didn't look over, but she could tell he was smiling.

She watched the speedometer needle slant to eighty-five, eighty-eight, and then ninety miles an hour. Harry stayed quiet. No warnings from his walkie-talkie either.

"I'm going home," she said forcefully, exhilaration churning through her. "Home. Dad will be calling us."

• • •

FBI

THE SNIPERS CEASED all movement and watched the dark-colored Cadillac drive slowly northward into the curve of the street, pull to the curb at the lamppost, and stop. The door opened. The dome light illuminated the interior of the car for maybe five seconds—no more.

Keeping low, resting his goggles on the top of the rise of dirt about two-tenths of a mile north, Agent Robinson clearly saw a blond woman, young, in bulky white clothes, lean low from the door and awkwardly toss a black bundle a few feet from the car to land beneath and against the streetlight.

"Good job," Agent Robinson whispered into the air. "Guy's got to go right under the light to get it." He and Bezick heard the metallic smack as the door swung shut with a force that suggested anger or fear. The tires spun gritty road dust into the air as the car sped off.

Robinson held the goggles on the black bag, describing it to Bezick as a soft, lumpy bundle about two feet by two feet. An Eddie Bauer label was facing up. A minute went by, two minutes. Bezick held the radio close to his partner's mouth, transmitting simultaneously to the assault unit on Reservation Road and Agent Ken Thompson at the operations center in San Jose. Another two minutes passed. Robinson's goggles were frozen on the bag.

Then, "Movement from the north, individual approaching bag," Robinson said quietly, keeping the goggles steady on the scene. "Subject running, crouched over. Losing him momentarily to underbrush and slopes on terrain."

In San Jose, the transmission from Robinson was clear, though Thompson had now lost the feeble link with LaFreniere. For the moment, he had only Robinson and the SWAT team lead on Reservation Road. He could hear both men breathing tight against their transmitters.

"Okay. Got him again." Agent Robinson picked up his hushed commentary. "Came through a break in the fence near the light post and picked up the bag. Running now, still crouching over, back through the fence, running north, losing him ... too foggy ... lost him. Has the dunes team spotted him?" Robinson's voice was low but edgy. "Any new orders for us? Still follow? Or take?"

"Hold there," said Thompson. "I'll be back." After one more maddening, failed attempt to reach either SAC Held, still hovering in the Huey, or Agent Tom LaFreniere, somewhere within a mile of Robinson and Bezick, Thompson decided. Full communication with command was essential, but the attempt to get it had just cost three more valuable minutes.

"Take him," Thompson said firmly. "Take the subject and get the bag."

Agents Robinson and Bezick left cover and raced onto the scrubby field of sand that stretched west about a quarter mile before the dunes rose to define the landscape and border the beach. Two other agents appeared from behind the ridge a few hundred yards north of them, and several more crossed over from the highway, followed by a second wave of men from cars or on foot from their observation posts surrounding the drop site. They fanned across the area where the snipers had last seen the subject running north with the black bag.

With the calm expertise of practice, the twenty-five or thirty men quickly formed a grid pattern across the expanse of sand and brush from the cul-de-sac to the dunes. They searched slowly north toward the remaining teams spread across the boundary at Del Monte Road.

Within half an hour, they found a pair of sneakers, still tied, tossed carelessly against a bush about four hundred yards north of Dunes Road: someone in a hurry who knew that bare feet were faster in sand. Not far beyond the shoes, the black duffel bag lay empty and crumpled. The searchers' infrared vision devices had picked up the winking "fireflies" that studded the bag to enable tracking.

Fifteen minutes later, a splintered shout bounced across the sand: "Over here!" A few of the searchers caught fragments of the voice distorted by the hissing surf a stone's throw to the west. They tracked the sound and found several agents squatting in a semicircle in the brush. They had found a discarded handgun.

"Looks like a standard .380 caliber semiautomatic," someone said. As with the sneakers and the black bag, no one moved or touched the pistol. One of the agents was already on the radio to the Evidence Recovery Team to report the location of the third piece of possible evidence. ERT would photograph, mark, and bag the items for storage until they would almost surely be called for in court.

The agents reassembled their grid and pressed on. The subject couldn't be far. They were literally breathing down his neck, forcing him northward into the net. Fog be damned—they'd get him.

• • •

Chuck

WHEN THE BASKETBALL game ended, Rock began flipping through the TV channels, so a wave of blurred voices and music and laugh tracks kept rolling into my corner. I tried to calculate the time. Steve had left to make the call to Kathy during the final quarter of the game, and televised NBA tournament games were usually over by ten o'clock. If we were somewhere close to ten, Kathy must be getting ready to bring the money.

She hadn't left my mind for one minute the whole evening, even though I could barely stand the thought of my little girl driving into this unknowable, unpredictable situation to help me. I knew Kathy. She would be brave and determined, wouldn't make a single complaint. I could almost hear her dry voice saying, "C'mon, I'm ready, let's do this thing." But she would be scared to death. *Protect her, Lord.*

Rock abruptly turned the television off and, as far as I could tell, did not get up or even shift in his seat. He said nothing, and his constant sniffing ceased. After hours of the familiar din of TV background noise, the silence was absolute. It unnerved me. For all I knew, he had his ubiquitous gun trained on my forehead. I tried to slouch further, dropping my head toward my knees.

We maintained that silent standoff for several minutes before I heard a car door slam and Steve walked in—toward me. He stood so close I could feel the toe of his shoe skimming my calf. "It's after ten o'clock, and I'm leaving now. If everything goes right, this could all be over by midnight. I'll be back an hour or two after that, and you could be free. If I'm not back by 4:00 AM, something's wrong."

"I'm sure everything will go exactly as you planned it," I told him, wanting very much for him to succeed tonight. It was my best hope, though I wasn't at all sure they would let me go after they got the money. I had seen Steve's face, however briefly. I was a liability now. Were they smart enough to remember that, or would they be too distracted by the cash?

"As long as they don't do anything stupid," he muttered.

"They won't. I know them," I said. "My family won't take a chance with my life."

"We'll see," Steve said darkly. Even without seeing him, I would have sworn he was glaring at me, bulging out his eyes for emphasis.

"You made a smart decision about using the Cadillac to bring you the money," I told him, trying to keep him positive. His conviction that he had masterminded a successful plot could be Kathy's best security.

I was also glad I had convinced him in an earlier conversation that she should stay in the car and drop the money in a visible place on the road. That was the day he considered having her walk onto the beach with the money. I shuddered again, remembering. It was intolerable to me that Kathy would be so alone and so vulnerable on a dark beach at midnight, walking into the possible trap of a criminal. In some weak way, I felt I had helped to protect my child.

Thank you, God, for giving me the words to convince him. And for seeing to it that he listened to me.

I heard Steve collecting things from around the room. Then he stopped in front of me and destroyed the shred of influence I naively thought I'd gained. "You better remember you'll be alone with Rock," he said in a tone saturated with self-importance. "He's very nervous tonight, very agitated. He's a violent man, so don't try anything. No fast moves or noises. He has a gun, and I don't know what he'll do."

Steve's footsteps moved away from me. With no idea where the words or the spirit behind them came from, I called out after him: "I'll pray for you—that you'll be successful tonight."

My words trailed outside as the front door opened. Steve's final warning about Rock lingered inside, taunting me, and the fear I carried in my belly began to crawl up toward my throat. Rock must have followed Steve outside, because I head the low murmur of voices for a minute before the engine revved up. Moist night air from the open door wrapped around my head and filtered under the blindfold, cooling my sore eyes. Then Rock returned and with him the silence, broken at intervals by his chronic, staccato sniffs.

Time dragged. I no longer had a pattern of TV shows or meal breaks to give me an idea of the hour. The acid in my gut would roil and rise every time I pictured Kathy alone on the highway, brave, sad, burdened, and terrified. For once in these long days of keeping vigil, Rock left the radio off. I strained to hear traffic sounds. A car's approach might mean that Steve was back—and successful. They would have their money and let me go. But cars were distant and few.

I wanted to pray every pleading prayer I ever learned, prayers that would make God lean way over to hear me and hold me up. But, as before, I kept coming back to the Rosary and the *Memorare*. Bead after bead, Hail Mary after Hail Mary, counting out the ten prayers by pressing my fingers against my thighs. A Glory Be, an Our Father and on to the next string of ten.

I tried to fill my mind with meditations on the Mysteries of the Rosary—special events in the life of Jesus and Mary—but though I'd memorized and recited them time and again as a child, I couldn't summon a single one. So I summoned my family.

I assigned my dad to the first decade, and while I murmured the timeworn words, I filled my mind with pictures of Dad. Dad standing at the sink vigorously scrubbing at the black ink on his hands and under his fingernails after a long day of examining plates at the photoengraver shop ... Dad and Mother talking at the kitchen table ... Dad sternly reminding his only child that nothing—absolutely nothing and no exceptions—was more important than my faith in God and my education

For some unknown reason, I remembered a conversation between them about the merits of butter versus margarine. Must have been the late '40s or early '50s. Mother was suspicious of the unfamiliar softness of margarine, which prompted Dad to immediately question the hardness of butter!

I think he taught me that night how to come at a problem from a new side, to flip my thinking to solve a problem. I also think he wanted my practical, less flexible mother, and maybe me, to recognize that we can always create a problem if we look for one—so look for the benefits instead. My dad.

Pictures came faster as the decade of prayers wound down. The awe on Dad's face as he held Peter for the first time ... the pride and satisfaction shining through his sweat as he hammered and sawed to build shelves for our first Adobe office. As I searched his face in my mental album, I could see and almost touch the kindness and optimism that lit up his eyes. Dad would be devastated when—if ... I had run out of fingers. End of the first decade. *Blessed Mother, watch over Matt Geschke.*

The second decade was Nan. My center. My touchstone. I didn't have to reach back for pictures, since her face was always before me, practically painted on the inside of the blindfold. She'd had some bad times over the past few years, carrying the weight of her sister's brutal murder like a thorn in her mind and heart. For some of those years I feared I was losing her to the anger and anxiety that had her so firmly in their grip.

But Nan had a deep, rich vein of strength running through to her core. I could all at once see the keen challenge in her eyes, hear the quick laugh that reduced every problem we faced to something manageable. How I had relied on her all these years to understand the nuances, to see the practical side, to cut to the chase, to organize the mess, to dry the tears, to pick up the slack, to take the dare, to laugh it off. That was my Nancy. It was the Irish in her that I needed. She set me free to fly—and I did.

I have loved you, Nan McDonough. I have loved the family we made. I have loved the life we built together. Because of you, I have loved.

A noise. A car. I straightened and cocked my head toward the door, straining my ears. I suddenly noticed that Rock had stopped his incessant pacing. I wanted nothing more than to hear Steve push through the door a few feet away, bragging about being rich. I prayed furiously that he would be crazy with high spirits and goodwill, maybe drunk. That he would love his wealth and success so much he would cut these cords and shove me into the night. *Yes! Please!*

Frozen in my rigid posture, barely breathing in anticipation, I heard the car roll slowly by; the street must have been only a few yards from where I sat. I heard a slight squeak of brakes. A car door slammed. A woman laughed. And then the car rolled slowly by again, the low rumble of engine and the soft slap of tires promptly fading.

Rock resumed his pacing in a maddening pattern. I didn't like Rock's growing agitation, so I breathed in deeply and exhaled long, hoping to stay calm. Where was Steve? What time was it? How long before Rock lost his patience and took it out on me? I pulled my mind back to the Rosary.

Where was I? Three more decades. Three kids. Ten Hail Marys apiece. Satisfied to have a mathematical method for getting through the next ten minutes, I thought about Peter, our oldest. The quintessential good guy. Strong and smart. Compassionate. Spontaneous. More romantic than analytical, though he was a damn fine mathematician. A math teacher, even. What I thought I would be.

Pigheaded, too, that son of mine. My heart caught remembering the night we argued about the courses he was choosing his final year in college. Not tough enough, I nagged. You're sliding, you're lazy. Work harder, do better, do more. In my own frustration, I pushed and pushed until, red-faced with anger, Peter jumped up from the table, slammed the door, started his car, and drove off. We didn't hear from him for three days.

Nan and I were sick with worry. I was devastated, full of remorse. How could a father drive away a son whom he loved beyond imagining? Why had I not heard him out? Listened to his reasoning? Tried to see his point of view? I made that kind of listening a policy in my company; why not in my family?

When Peter returned on the fourth day and calmly strode into the kitchen for dinner, I had grabbed him, hugged him—and cried. I have never since felt such a depth of sorrow and loss, even as I grew more certain that I would die this night.

I whispered the Lord's Prayer audibly, imagining the single bead that separated the sets of Hail Marys. I was beyond caring if Rock shouted at me. Fortunately, he ignored me, preoccupied with his anxiety over Steve's return. I heard the door open and close periodically. Checking the street for signs of Steve, I guessed. I had a sense it was late, much later than Steve had planned to be back.

Lord God, please don't let anything go wrong. Let them win. My little girl is in the midst of it. Keep her safe. I'd rather die than have them harm her. You can't let that happen—please, Lord!

I had to keep my mind off Kathy. Next decade. I trudged on. From Peter to John, our youngest. John was our burn-the-candle-at-both-ends guy: fun and athletic with off-the-chart intelligence.

John was in high school when our economic circumstances changed dramatically with the success of Adobe, and we worried more about him than the others. We were determined to keep him rooted in the traditional ethic of hard work, thrift, and wise judgment that was ingrained in us through the example of our parents. Like personal freedom, material wealth was a responsibility as well as a blessing.

I think John got the message. It must have been his senior year. I can still see him standing in our bedroom that night after a classmate's party—handsome, cool, and a little cocksure. "I have to tell you something," he said. No big deal, he told us, but there was some alcohol at the party, and somehow the Los Altos police got wind of it, and somehow he was one of the kids "in possession."

Well, it *was* a big deal to his father! I restricted the poor kid to the house for the rest of the school year—his senior year. He could come and go to school only. Must have been nearly four months. John went nuts at first. Nan thought the punishment overbalanced the crime. John spent hours and days on end watching TV with Grandpa Matt, helping around the house, reading, and generally staying mad at me.

I felt awful for him and awful for myself. But all I could think of was the awesome weight of responsibility a father has. If this talented, popular boy was to become the kind of man I knew he could be, he had to learn accountability. And I was accountable to him for his progress into maturity.

My eyes began to sting again when I remembered the day a couple of years later when John told me, "I hated you for it then, Dad, but I respected the guts it took to follow it through. I still do. You taught me what responsibility means."

I was nearly out of prayers—and then what? I was too tired to think of new ways to outsmart the kidnappers. It was too late. Nothing was happening. If Steve didn't get back, Rock would kill me and disappear. *The Rosary, Chuck. Stay with the Rosary.*

The last decade was for Kathy. I'd been meditating on her for four days now, my brave girl. What a confident little gal she was as a child, too. Always a big-picture, broad-stroke person—but organized, despite that. An intriguing combination of talents that Nan and I both marveled at. Great spatial vision: give her an empty wall or room, and she would transform it into art by selecting and arranging fabric and furniture and artwork. She got the artistic talent from Nan, who could draw and paint like a professional, though she had little training. I was hopeless in that department. And Kathy was hopeless with numbers.

We still talk about that notorious geometry test her sophomore year in high school. I wouldn't accept a low grade in geometry, I told her. She was as smart as any other student and she could—and would—understand it. I left her no option. When she moaned and groaned and struggled with her homework, I tutored patiently. Night after night, I demonstrated, I explained, I diagrammed. Kathy simply studied. On the day of the big test, I felt she was ready. I don't remember asking her what *she* felt.

The next night, when she reluctantly handed me her D—or was it an F?—her sorrow was so obvious and so profound that I was struck with insight. The pressure for my daughter wasn't about learning the math; it was her fear of disappointing *me*. How could I have put such a heavy burden on my child's shoulders? How much did I demand of her love for me?

I shoved the offensive paper aside and showered my daughter with praise for her dedication and determination. How could she ever disappoint me, I wondered then. And now, I had done it again. Put impossible pressure on Kathy's shoulders where failing the test could not just disappoint her father, it could kill him.

Oh, Kathy. I am so sorry, my sweet girl. I am full of admiration and gratitude for the journey you are making for me tonight. I am sorry I couldn't tutor you or tease you through it. In fact, I was no help to you at all, was I? There is no grade but A tonight,

Kathy. Whatever happens, your effort and your love are enough for me.

I was just beginning the final *Memorare*, putting all my beloved family, one by one, into the care of the Virgin Mary, when an alarm bell jangled so loudly that my head slammed back against the wall and my heart hammered instantly and violently against my ribs. "What's that?" I gasped, disoriented.

"It's 4:00 AM," growled Rock.

"What does that mean?" As I said the words, I remembered Steve's parting conversation with Rock. He would be back around 2:00 AM, he said. If it got as late as four o'clock, something was wrong.

"Something's gone wrong," Rock said in an abstract way he hadn't used before, as though he were confirming to himself what he feared but expected. The room was still, and I could almost feel the strain of Rock's indecision. Without Steve's leadership—without Steve—he was lost. No partner, no money, no escape.

He wound the portable alarm clock in strong, jerky bursts of motion. "Thirty minutes more," he muttered. "Then I go and do it myself." I was suddenly chilled by the thought of Rock's power over me. If Steve didn't return, Rock would have no choice but to eliminate me and get the hell out. And he would do it soon. The ticking of the clock was loud in the small silent room.

A flash of inspiration made the dots before my blinded eyes speed up and collide. The mastermind was gone, and the plan was in jeopardy. Maybe there was opportunity for me in Rock's doubt. Could I wedge the crack wider?

"That's strange. He said he'd be back around 2:00 AM, didn't he?" I tried to discreetly build on Rock's doubt.

"So what? Lots of reasons someone is late," Rock said, quickly defensive.

"Yeah. True." I waited a minute before I added, "Must be a great feeling for Steve to finally have all that money in his pocket. How much are you getting again?"

"Three hundred thousand. Half." I could almost see him licking his lips. This was my chance.

"You trust him?"

That got Rock's attention. All of a sudden he was only inches away from me. I could dimly discern the curve of his shoe near my leg and feel his breath on my shoulder. "What are you saying? What do you mean?" he spat out.

"Nothing, really, except that it would be easy for Steve to collect all the money and then just drive off and disappear, wouldn't it? He made all the phone calls, too. How do you know he didn't really ask for more?"

Rock said nothing, just breathed in and out loudly.

"All I'm saying is that I would guess he got a lot more money than six hundred thousand dollars. Or that he plans to keep it all for himself. Why not? You're not there to watch him. I could be wrong, though."

"He wouldn't cheat me. He wouldn't cheat me," Rock repeated in that same detached voice he used earlier. I hoped it meant I had confused him and made him doubt Steve. If I could create conflict between them, they might forget about me in dealing with each other.

Rock jerked into action, kicking the chains closer to me and pulling my leg forward. He clamped one end tightly to my ankle, wove the rest across and through my legs, ending with the clamp on the other foot. He checked my wrist shackles and tightened my blindfold, though the fabric still allowed faint light beneath my eyes.

"The clamps are pinching my ankles pretty bad. Can you loosen them up a little bit?"

"No," Rock answered from a different position somewhere across the room.

They hurt, so I pressed the point. "Please. They're cutting off the blood flow."

To keep me from nagging him, he stood over me, lifted the chains, and jiggled them. When I yelped, he bent down and very slightly loosened one of the clamps. It wasn't much, and they still hurt, but it was a concession. He apparently saw some value in keeping me alive for a while longer.

About ten minutes later, the alarm sounded again. This time I was wide awake and ready for it. "Now what," I said, shifting under the weight of the chains.

"I'm going to find him," Rock said in a dead voice.

"And if you don't?" My brain sent me a dull warning that I ignored. I couldn't stop myself from asking.

"Then it's time for Plan B," he said, surprisingly close to my ear. Unprepared, I flinched.

"What's Plan B?" I asked him, again suppressing the brain signal to stop talking.

"You don't want to know." He left, slamming the door behind him.

SATURDAY | MAY 30

· MORNING ·

FBI

THE FBI'S grid-pattern search of the beach continued into the early morning hours, long after Kathy Geschke had spun out of the Dunes Road cul-de-sac on her way back to Los Altos, focused on nothing but the promised release of her father. The perimeter tightened as the men on the beach moved systematically northward to meet the rest of their team on Del Monte Road. Within their net, every potential exit from the beach to the highway had been monitored since the drop took place just before midnight. There was no doubt their target was trapped somewhere inside that rough square mile. But progress was measured and cautious, with every agent acutely aware that an armed felon could be hiding in any gully, any copse of shrubs, any rack of trees.

As the Evidence Recovery Team moved in to bag the handgun, shoes, duffel bag and binoculars turned up by the federal beachcombers near the drop site, Agent Larry Taylor and his partner drove to the cement plant situated about halfway between Dunes and Del Monte, the natural midpoint on the projected escape route. The twenty-four-hour sand and gravel operation meant a crew was on duty and may have seen something odd or helpful.

"Nooo, nothin' unusual 'round here tonight." The worker respond-ed to Taylor's questioning with careful deliberation, finally shaking his head. "Nope. Don't think so."

Regardless of how they framed their questions, the agents got much the same response from all four workers on the night shift. Bottom line: the men were "sure sorry we can't help y'out." Agent Taylor thanked them and walked rapidly to the car. No sense wasting more time on a dead end.

As he was about to turn over the ignition, one of the factory crew suddenly called out, "Oh, wait now ... nothing *real* unusual except for this guy that came by a few minutes before you and asked for a ride to the highway. Said he'd pay us five hundred bucks for a ride out. We thought he was a nutcase, coming in from the beach at this hour. Told him no. Couldn't leave the plant anyway."

"Just now?" Taylor was out of the car in an instant. "What'd he look like? Where'd he go?"

"Lemme see ... short, thin guy. Tannish skin. Dark clothes. And no shoes, either." As he spoke, the man lifted his finger to point toward the rear of the plant, toward the beach. At almost the same moment, Taylor and his partner sprinted past him into the darkness beyond.

In less than a minute, the two agents discovered fresh prints of bare feet in the wet sand. As they reverse-tracked the prints back to the surf line, Taylor radioed for urgent SWAT team reinforcement at the cement plant. Several of the agents participating in the north-pressing grid search were already nearing the cement plant and ar-rived at Taylor's location within ten minutes. Along with Taylor and his partner, the agents followed the prints about two hundred feet inland to the edge of a freshwater dune pond banked by logs and bristly vegetation.

Despite night vision equipment and state-of-the-art, handheld searchlights, the footprints were lost to the dense undergrowth lead-ing into acres of flat sand and farm fields away from the pond and the shore. Their man was heading inland, with plenty of thickets and tree stands to hide him, not to mention his advantage of a cloudy, moonless night with almost three hours to go before light would break in the east.

Taylor sat wearily on the end of a stout log protruding from the sand near the pond and radioed the Marina command post that he'd be coming in. The SWAT detail would continue to press the grid up the beach.

Toward daybreak, thanks to the slowly dissolving fog, military helicopters took to the air to lend support to the chase. Agent Tom LaFreniere, who was directing the operation from Del Monte Road, had requested the chopper pilots to conduct a bridge search. The low, slow, back-and-forth flight pattern would move south from Del Monte, covering every inch of land until it overlapped with the ground search.

With the arrival of the choppers and the broad-sweep backup they provided, LaFreniere was able to pull some of his men from the marshland and artichoke fields south of Del Monte. His teams had been on standby alert, surveillance, observation, or search detail for more than twelve hours without a break. Now he could set up shifts, let some of them get food and a little rest. They'd need it since he had no intention of halting the search to wait for daylight, as the tactical command post had suggested.

Command believed the target was lost. Agent LaFreniere and his men refused to believe it. They refused to abandon the search even for a few hours, convinced the target was under their noses. He escaped their net once—an embarrassment—but it wouldn't happen again. For LaFreniere and his SWAT teams, there was no option but to stay in place until they flushed their man.

The low drone of the choppers blended into the muffled drum of the surf as LaFreniere and two fellow agents watched the sky go from dark gray to violet to rose in the east. It was six o'clock Saturday morning, six hours after the drop.

Still alert, thanks in part to frequent, generous cups of coffee, LaFreniere turned his head slowly in a routine visual sweep. He locked his gaze on the tree line that cut across the field and ran perpendicular to the strip of dirt road where the government vehicles had parked through the night. After it crossed Route 1, Del Monte became the unpaved access road to the nature preserve that extended to the west beyond them.

LaFreniere was staring, sipping cold coffee and lost in formulating a new search plan when he caught a small movement at the edge of the tree line. He sat up straight and trained his binoculars. Something small and dark was emerging from the woods toward the highway about two hundred feet from his vehicle. He watched. As the figure came closer, he clearly observed a lone man with dark clothing, a slight build, and an olive complexion. The subject was barefoot and slightly limping. The man's appearance mirrored the description Taylor had radioed in from the cement plant four hours earlier.

"Has to be him," LaFreniere muttered, both relief and adrenalin flooding through him. He trailed the man slowly in the car for a minute or two, eventually drawing alongside him. LaFreniere left his vehicle and approached the subject who made no attempt to run. He appeared wet, disheveled, cold, and tired.

The subject didn't react when Agent LaFreniere showed his badge and explained they were investigating a kidnapping case in the area and needed to ask him a few questions. Nor did he resist when the agent nudged him against the car to search for identification and a weapon. LaFreniere called in the driver's license ID: "Albukhari," he reported to the command post. "Guy says his first name's Mouataz, goes by Mo."

"Hold him, Tom," came the prompt order from the field command. "Same name on the gun we found. We're on our way."

Agent LaFreniere was elated. With the last name on the driver's license matching the name on the gun registration, there was little doubt they had their man. Further, the body search turned up a receipt for a room the night before at the Motel 6 on Dunes Road. Still, LaFreniere didn't make an arrest. When a human life was at stake in a crime under investigation, an arrest wasn't necessary to detain a suspect for questioning. So they'd do an interview first. Maybe he'd lead them to Geschke.

With the morning light rapidly brightening the sky, LaFreniere and the man who could be the closest connection they had to Chuck Geschke waited together inside the FBI vehicle for Agent Larry Taylor who had already been dispatched to Del Monte Road. Taylor's orders were to pick up the suspect and conduct the first interview. The overriding objective? Find Geschke.

Taylor arrived from the Marina command post in a matter of minutes. A respected veteran of criminal interviews, Taylor assessed Albukhari as he led him to his car. Guy's exhausted, worried, but not too scared yet, Taylor decided. Naïve, though. Still thinking he can get out of this and calculating how to do it. Out of his league and doesn't know it.

Taylor steered the man into the backseat and climbed in next to him, the agent's stocky, muscular physique contrasting sharply with the slight, slender frame of the suspect. While his partner drove back to the motel room near the drop site, Taylor began talking casually— almost conversationally—about the recent abduction of a Mr. Charles Geschke. Mr. Albukhari repeatedly denied involvement and gave little useful information: he hadn't heard anything about a kidnapping, the gun was on loan from his brother, he had come to Monterey on a scuba diving trip—check with his wife.

Taylor let him run on with his fabricated stories. Experience told him that most suspects gradually catch themselves up; stories often begin to break down in the details as the agents keep up a gentle probing on the case in point, never saying outright that the detainee is a suspect.

While he spoke about the Geschke crime, the pain of the family, the fear for all their lives, Taylor placed his hand on the back of the exhausted Mr. Albukhari's neck, massaging slowly. *Where the hell did this tactic come from?* Taylor asked himself as they drove back to Dunes Road, surprised and amused by his choice of a technique so out of character for him. But something told him the soft approach was right. It seemed to calm and disarm the suspect.

If the neck kneading didn't work, something did. Seated in Albukhari's motel room, Agent Taylor once again talked about a kidnapping, adroitly steering his story around any technicalities that might compromise a court case, should Mr. Albukhari confess.

They talked about a generic kidnapping, a generic trial, and the range of possible punishments for criminals convicted of kidnapping. The suspect listened more intently when the topic turned to trials and sentencing. It was late morning, nearly 11:00 when, finally, Mr. Albukhari interrupted with a question: "What sentence would you get if you did something like that?"

Larry Taylor understood timing and opportunity—and this was it. Keeping his voice low and amiable, he replied with a direct question and command: "Where is Mr. Geschke? Tell us."

Albukhari was silent. No protest. No denial. The silence stretched and deepened until the faint rumble of surf could be heard from beyond the dunes. Finally, the man spoke weakly, warily. "I'll tell you, if you will ... "

Bingo! Negotiation. The suspect was angling for a deal. Taylor looked at his partner with satisfaction. There was still a chance to find Geschke.

• • •

Chuck

THE RADIO was loud. The blaring volume assaulted my hypersensitive ears to the point of pain. I wanted to stomp on it or slam it against a wall to stop the incessant drumming beat. But I could barely get my cuffed hands up to cover my ears, much less find a way around the floor posts and then drag my chained legs across a room to find the radio. Truth was, I wasn't just mad about the radio. I was angry and frustrated and fearful to the point of despair.

My attempt to escape while Rock was gone had been a travesty. He'd been on foot, barely a block away, and had spotted me the moment I turned the corner. I was weaponless and no match for the hefty knife he was carrying. I had gained nothing but tighter chains and new fear. I still felt the band of nausea ripple in my gut when I recalled what I saw near the front door when I first got free.

I had recognized my briefcase right away. What turned my stomach was the message crudely scraped into the leather with a sharp tool like a penknife: "CG is dead." The concrete evidence that my captors planned all along to kill me struck me with the force of a boxer's blow. The constant verbal threats had scared me senseless, but this was concrete proof. The mental blindfold was off.

It had been a couple of hours since Rock left for the second time. Furious about my escape, he chained me tighter than ever and punched up the radio, figuring the volume would cover any noise I could make from yelling or kicking at the closet door. But I wouldn't try anymore. Not one neighbor had looked outside when Rock pushed me down the street at knifepoint after he grabbed me at the corner. They wouldn't come to the door to investigate loud music either. No one cared.

All of a sudden the room went quiet. I lifted my head and listened as carefully as a dog on point. No music. No radio. I heard a few footsteps. Someone was standing in front of my closet. The door was partially open and in the narrow band of light, I could see part of a shoe beneath my blindfold: a black running shoe with the Nike logo.

The voice was unfamiliar, higher and crisper than Rock's or Steve's though accented in the same way. A third man! "I'm the leader of this organization, Mr. Geschke," the man said. "The others have screwed up, so I'm going to arrange for your release. I'll be taking you to a different part of the state in a little while."

He walked away and a door closed. Had he left already? Was he really coming back? Had he done something to Rock? A couple of days ago, I might have considered it a hopeful sign, but I didn't believe anything anymore.

I'm tired of hoping. It's too late. All I want now is to stay inside my mind where I can talk to God and see pictures of my family. That's the only safe place. Remember, oh most gracious Virgin Mary ...

The worn words of the *Memorare* came to me automatically, and their rhythm pulled me toward a numbing sleep. *I'm ready.*

• • •

FBI

AFTER HE made the arrest, it wasn't hard for Taylor to convince Albukhari that things would go better for him and his defense if he cooperated. Even better if the hostage was unharmed. But to get any deal, he had to lead them to Geschke first—now. Taylor thought the guy seemed willing enough, though he said he couldn't remember the name of the small town up the highway where his partner was guarding Geschke and waiting for Albukhari in a "safe house."

Taylor was troubled, though. The guy wasn't giving any ground on the money. Dropped it while he was running, couldn't remember where or when, he said. Then—wait, no. He suddenly remembered tossing it into the surf so he wouldn't be caught with it.

Taylor didn't buy it either way. The meticulous grid search, along with the dogs, metal detectors, and electronic vision devices would have turned up even a dime carelessly tossed on the beach or on the acres of flat land fronting the dunes. And pitching it into the water didn't make sense, although the guy's pants were wet up to the thigh when he'd walked out of the woods. Taylor was positive their man hid it and was still harboring the crazy idea that he'd somehow get out of this mess and return to claim his prize.

But recovering the money was secondary. Getting to Mr. Geschke was the only focus now. Albukhari sketched out a rough map, remembering that he took Highway 1 about five miles up to Interstate 101, then got off the 101 at the next exit—about five more miles, he thought—and then headed east for about fifteen miles to the town.

Agent Taylor called the coordinates in to field command. In minutes, they were back. Puts us in Hollister, they said. The suspect agreed that "Hollister" sounded right and gave them an address: Number 5 Hodel Court. Taylor radioed command again.

Action was immediate. The choppers were dispatched first with sniper teams on board under orders to set up surveillance from rooftop and street positions surrounding the address on Hodel Court. Remaining SWAT teams, evidence recovery teams, and surveillance operations groups were notified and ordered to temporarily suspend the search for the money and converge on Hollister prepared for a possible raid, a possible rescue, or a possible takedown.

A lengthy caravan of FBI vehicles and police cars hustled onto Highway 1 in a curling black line that invaded the fast lane. For the first time since the abduction, they had a mission with clarity.

They planned for hostage rescue. They would send Albukhari inside the house to engage his partner. SWAT teams in black FBI jackets and balaclava—black hoods with eyeholes—were already in position around the perimeter. Some encircled the house; others bordered the square block surrounding Hodel Court.

Between 12:30 and 1:00 PM, the motorcade of utilitarian black Fords arrived in Hollister and quietly surrounded the little alley, keeping off the street itself. The car carrying Taylor and the suspect parked at the entry to the short street.

With dozens of eyes following his progress, Albukhari was dispatched down the block about fifty feet to the doorway of number 5 with orders to bring his partner outside. There was no fear he would bolt. The perimeter was so tight, he would be netted in seconds. And by now he was keenly aware that cooperation might mitigate his punishment.

Albukhari unlocked the door and pushed inside. Forty law enforcement officers outside were ready for anything. Any kind of eruption at the door would be met with an instant raid of the SWAT team. When Albukhari reappeared and called out, "He's gone!" the SWATs thundered past him through the narrow doorway, guns drawn, shouting the standard language of the raid: *"GET DOWN. GET DOWN. FBI. GET DOWN. FBI."*

The agents swept the rooms to search and secure the site. Almost at once another shout carried to the street: "Bound man in bedroom closet." The moment the entry team declared the site secure, Agent Taylor, who had followed the team in, was allowed to enter the bedroom. From here on, he was responsible for the victim.

Taylor was cautious as he approached the closet. He recognized Chuck Geschke at once from the photos circulated among the agents. But the man was curled in on himself, in a near fetal position, mute and trembling.

Taylor understood the signs. He could barely imagine what the man would be feeling after days of being blindfolded, threatened, and chained, then suddenly interrupted by the alarming pandemonium of a takedown entry—a tactic designed to stun, intimidate, and terrorize in order to gain a few seconds of advantage. The shock could be paralyzing.

The first thing the man needed was reassurance. Taylor wanted him to first feel a nonthreatening human touch. He knelt beside the blindfolded hostage and placed both hands lightly on his face. "Mr. Geschke? I'm Larry Taylor, and I'm with the FBI."

Chuck stirred and sat up, rattling the huge chains that encircled his legs and lower body. In a throaty voice full of skepticism and fight, he said, "I don't believe you!"

Taylor admired the belligerence still evident in this beleaguered man, obviously pushed to his limit and beyond. Taylor chuckled and said again, "It's true. I'm Special Agent Larry Taylor with the FBI. We're going to take you home, sir."

Taylor reached out to remove the duct tape blindfold, wincing when he saw Geschke's full beard, now overgrown and shaggy. "It's gonna hurt, sir," he said, still kneeling in front of him. Trying to be gentle, Taylor fumbled at the corners of the sticky strip, tugging slowly. He knew it would first have a biting sting and then burn like fire.

But Taylor was too slow for Chuck who, despite his handcuffs, managed to get hold of a strip Taylor had loosened and yank it with determination, pulling the whole thing off. Tissue-like bits of skin and small tufts of hair came with it, but after an initial yelp, Geschke barely seemed to notice. Still distrustful, Chuck pulled himself up straighter, glared at Larry Taylor, and demanded, "Let me see your badge!"

"Sure thing, Mr. Geschke." Agent Taylor showed his credentials. Glancing from the badge back to Taylor's face and then to the scene unfolding around him, Chuck began to nod slowly. Taylor stepped back. It would take Geschke a few minutes to fully trust this new reality.

Men in black ninja suits were still roaming the rooms, garage, and backyard of the small house, guns drawn.

A couple of the men bent over Geschke and unlocked the leg chains and handcuffs with a master key.

Taylor, much less menacing in an ordinary business suit, helped Geschke to his feet and supported him as he shook the stiffness from his legs and hips. Together, they slowly made their way through the front door to the street, which was packed with milling police, FBI agents, government vehicles, and neighbors.

Still wobbly and dazed, Chuck shook his head, as if disbelieving that the churning activity in the street was related to him and his dramatic rescue. Taylor held him firmly by the elbow, elated to be watching Geschke's gradual realization that his ordeal was truly over and that the men and women surrounding him were his advocates, his defenders—his freedom!

Still surveying the scene in amazement, Geschke relaxed little by little and began to smile. Taylor guided him through the commotion toward Special Agent in Charge Dick Held, who was leaning against one of the black government cars, talking on a radio.

Wading through a sea of agents in black windbreakers with the bold yellow block letters "FBI" on the back, Geschke recovered his balance—and his wit. "I thought angels were supposed to wear white," he quipped as he passed. "You guys sure are *my* angels, but you're all dressed in black!"

"We thought you might want to make a phone call, sir," said Taylor, smiling. "Our operation commander here is going to connect with our agent at your house first to let her know you'll be on the phone. Bear with us a minute."

"Damn! We're not getting a signal," muttered one of the agents on the communications team who was holding a boxy portable phone taken from an FBI vehicle. SAC Held frowned and reached for the phone to try for himself.

"Geez," said a teasing voice behind him in a stage whisper. "Our transmitters fail, our choppers can't land, our radios go out ... and now the doggone phones don't work!"

"Yup. And we *still* get a rescue and an arrest," said someone else over a spate of good-natured laughter. Despite their exasperation with the string of technology challenges over the past few days, relief and good humor overrode the Bureau's tendency to self-reproach. After all, they had proof of a successful operation standing right in front of them.

"Got a phone for you, Mr. Geschke," said another agent, reaching into the center of the group to hand a different phone to SAC Held. The agent had noticed and borrowed the portable phone of a neighbor who, incredibly, continued to wash his car in the midst of the drama in the little alley.

SAC Held dialed again and connected. He turned aside to conduct a brief conversation with the agent on the other end. Then he held out the phone to Chuck. Chuck's hands trembled as he took the phone. No one in his family knew yet that he was safe.

• • •

Chuck

Who will answer first? Will Kathy snatch up the phone as she did countless times as a teenager? Will it be Peter's relaxed, alto "hello" or John's cool, laconic "what's up?" Or will it be Nan's warm, inquisitive voice and the quick, light laugh I thought I'd never hear again? Are they all there? Waiting still? Did they call John home from school? My mind races into the few seconds of silence on the other end of the line.

Suddenly Nan's voice, breaking and breathless. Saying my name over and over, pulling me toward her. I can barely talk through the tremor in my voice, barely see through the welling of my eyes. "Nan, I love you. Kathy? Pete? John? It's Dad. Is everyone okay? I'm coming home." The urgency to see them and touch them overwhelms me.

• • •

FBI

AFTER THE BRIEF CONTACT with his family, the FBI hustled Chuck Geschke to one of the Vietnam-era helicopters waiting on Hollister's San Benito High School playing fields a few blocks away. According to protocol, he would be debriefed by the Bureau in San Jose and later by the police in Mountain View, within whose jurisdiction the crime occurred.

As they took off for San Jose, Agent Larry Taylor sat alone and apart on the floor of the chopper, eyes closed and lips slightly moving in a silent prayer of thanksgiving for the safe rescue of Charles Geschke. The line between life and death was so fragile. Taylor knew that if the chain of events had been slightly different in even one of a hundred ways, this decent man could have died a violent death and left his family devastated.

In so much of Taylor's work, death hovered over him and the people he had vowed to protect. But often, the Bureau and the skilled men and women he worked with were able to snatch a victory from violence and death. The veteran agent was grateful.

· AFTERNOON ·

Nan

THE PHONE RANG about 1:00 PM after a lunch nobody had eaten. Marva and I were halfheartedly putting sandwiches in baggies and covering salad bowls with foil. Since it was still possible the kidnapper would call, Mary Ellen was answering all calls on the house phone, and we paid no attention as she walked over to the kitchen from the adjoining den where she was sitting with Kathy. Besides, by now we had no hope it was word of Chuck.

As the morning hours had dragged on, our small group of friends, Mary Ellen O'Toole, and a couple other FBI agents became more and more dispirited. There was no news. Kathy hardly moved or spoke. Exhaustion hung over her like a veil as she stared vacantly at the phone or out the window. Peter frightened me with his uncharacteristic loss of optimism. He said little and walked restlessly from room to room. About 5:00 that morning, he had suddenly dropped to the floor in anguish, utterly convinced that his father was dead.

As I watched my vibrant, precious children slowly dissolve into heart-wrenching grief, I could think only that I had failed them. I'd been unable to shield them from this misery and pain. Though my rational side told me this could not be so, I could think only as a mother who wanted desperately to take away her children's pain. My own pain I shoved into a distant, dark room of my brain, trying to ignore its howling demand to get out.

No one had slept all night, including Kathy, who was so agitated when she returned from the drop that I once thought I could see her heart bumping against the wall of her chest. Mostly, we paced, prayed, and drank endless cups of coffee and tea. We all stayed together in the living room, talking quietly, often brooding, but now and then finding something to lift our spirits. Though he had no updates, John Warnock touched base with the Adobe management team periodically, while Marva kept us all grounded by reminding us to eat and rest.

Mary Ellen had stayed at our sides throughout the night, too. Kathy's bond with this impressive woman had grown so strong that Kathy begged her not to leave. I was certain she would have stayed anyway. It was obvious to me that Mary Ellen cared about us as a family—not just as victims. She was the calm, confident leader we all relied on. To Kathy, she had become a sister.

About 3:00 AM, after taking a long phone call in the study, Mary Ellen had told us what she knew. She crossed into the living room— reluctantly, I thought. But at that point, we were still full of hope; maybe too hopeful to read anxiety in her eyes or hear unease in her voice, too hopeful to recognize that if she brought *good* news, she would be rushing in and smiling with delight.

"What's up? Have they found him? What did they tell you?" We had all jumped up and talked at once, our weariness buried in animation.

"Well ... " Mary Ellen began, "I don't know how to tell you this, but ... but we lost the kidnapper and the money in the fog." She pressed her lips together and turned away for a minute. Something in me sensed the effort it cost Mary Ellen to give us that news. I went cold inside with the implications.

Kathy gave a little cry. "Oh, no. No!"

Mary Ellen had turned back and looked at us squarely, once again poised and resolute. She smiled slightly and rushed on. "But there's no call to lose hope. There are lots of good things happening. Agents are still out there combing every inch of the beach. They have a net around every possible escape route. There's no doubt we'll find him. And once we have him, we as good as have Mr. Geschke."

She had added with warmth, "Just keep hoping and praying like you have been. You're a strong, strong family. You have to do the hoping for all of us, because the FBI doesn't operate on hope. We *fix* it; we don't *hope* to fix it. There's no option for us. So believe." She smiled at us again, gave Kathy's shoulders a fond squeeze, and left the room.

Her words had sounded to me like a standard speech for when things were going wrong. What did Mary Ellen really think? Did *she* have hope? I had seen the disappointment in her eyes. Even so, I trusted Mary Ellen. I chose to believe her.

But that was hours ago. Now, at just past 1:00 PM, the temporary distraction of lunch was over, and the long afternoon stretched ahead like an incurable illness. Marva and I finished up in the kitchen and trekked back to the living room to keep watch with the others. Mary Ellen was still talking on the kitchen phone, and Kathy waited for her in the den. As usual, Mary Ellen's voice behind us was low and even, as though taking a routine report. No emotion. It could not be good news.

I thought about going upstairs to be alone but was still drowsing in the living room when I heard Kathy cry out. Alarmed and filled with dread, I jumped upright just as Mary Ellen hurried toward me from the kitchen, phone in her outstretched hand. Kathy, standing beside her, was shaking and sobbing. But Mary Ellen was smiling.

"I think someone wants to speak with you, Mrs. Geschke," she said, gesturing to me with the receiver.

I began to shake my head, now buzzing with the effort to put the signals together. I clamped my hand to my mouth. The throbbing confusion of faith and fear began to hum with possibility. "Oh, no! Oh, God!"

I flew across the room toward Mary Ellen and, trembling, reached for the phone. Peter and the Warnocks rushed forward as well until all six of us were clustered around the smiling agent. Kathy, who must have immediately seen the triumph in Mary Ellen's shining face and brimming eyes, suddenly stepped back and began to laugh. My daughter laughing joyously while tears streamed down her face! Then I knew.

His voice was distant and patchy. I strained to hear over the static and background noise. "Chuck? Chuck? *CHUCK!*" I was shouting, shrieking his name over and over while laughing, crying, and trying to catch my breath all at the same time. Then, in a breath, he was gone. But his reassuring words encircled me like arms, ringing in my ears and echoing off the walls.

"He's alive. He's safe. He loves us. He's coming home," I told the weeping, hugging crowd of family and happy FBI agents who had gathered around me in the joyful noise. "Chuck's coming home!"

•   •   •

Chuck

Home. I'm going home. I keep repeating the word in my head as the street names outside the window of the government's Crown Victoria gradually become familiar. My FBI escorts fall silent.

We cross a cement bridge with its adjacent sign in small block letters: "Adobe Creek." Adobe. The clear, narrow stream meanders across the landscape as it probably has for centuries, oblivious to the dramatic role its name has played in my life. A left turn from El Camino onto University. Only a few blocks from the house.

And then, there they are, standing together in a front yard strung with banners. Nan, Kathy, Peter, and close behind them, Marva and John, cheering and waving wildly. As the car slows to a stop, I am suddenly swept through with such a delirious joy that I gasp at the power of it.

Now I'm close enough to see tears on every face, though their smiles are broad and joyful. I am close enough to see exhaustion and relief and worry lines not quite erased. Beautiful faces. Beloved faces. Then my own tears come so fast, I am momentarily blinded. The agent escort springs from the front seat and pulls open the back passenger door to release me.

I barely register the din of cheers and applause as I lunge forward, arms outstretched. I feel myself pulled hungrily into the warm, tight, laughing, crying embrace of my family and my friends. I cling to them fiercely. And somewhere in my head, there is a fleeting prayer of thanks. I must have turned right.

Epilogue

The Weekend

FOR THE REMAINDER of Saturday, Chuck Geschke sought neither rest nor privacy—only a shower and clean clothes. He asked his family to surround him with as many as possible of the people and voices he knew and loved. By 5:00 PM, the house was filled with friends. Peter had collected fiancée Diane and Grandpa Matt. Kathy's friends began to call and stop by. Friends, neighbors, and Adobe colleagues soon spilled from the house into the yard.

Deeply feeling their younger son's absence in the joyful reunion, Chuck and Nan placed a call to John, still in New Jersey, still camping in the woods, and still unaware of the nightmare his family had endured for the past five days. They were fearful that John would learn of Chuck's abduction through the media and would be not only shocked and worried, but also hurt and angry about being kept in the dark. They left word for John to call home immediately upon his return to his campus apartment.

Throughout the evening, Chuck spoke little of his own ordeal. Instead, he seemed to relish hearing the stories of those who lived the five-day span at his home or at Adobe.

Kathy, who had slept not at all since the ransom drop, sat quietly in the midst of the hubbub, a friend's year-old baby on her lap. With the little girl nestled close to her, Kathy seemed content. Nan and Peter circulated among the guests, trying to fill in the large gaps in their friends' knowledge of the events of the previous week. Both of them kept Chuck within clear sight and easy reach.

When the baby's family left, Kathy retreated to her bedroom where, finally, she could "sleep forever" as she had vowed to do when the ordeal was over. Chuck unfailingly left the party every half hour through midnight to climb the stairs and check on Kathy as she slept.

On Sunday, while Nan and Chuck—heavily guarded—attended Mass and prepared for a family dinner, the beach in Monterey was alive with activity. Special Agent Larry Taylor and the Evidence Recovery Team continued to comb the beach for the missing ransom money, equipped with mine-sweeper metal detectors on loan from the U.S. Army and issued from the ranger station at Marina Beach. About twenty feet offshore, Special Agent Tom LaFreniere's dive team in slick black wet suits was preparing to explore the sandy bottom in the area where the suspect claimed he had thrown the money into the water.

Less than an hour after the search began, a signal was picked up from the air. The reluctant transmitter buried inside the bundle of money had mysteriously come to life. It led the FBI recovery team back to the pond near the cement factory where they had lost the suspect's trail of footprints in the early hours of Saturday morning. The money was found wedged into a deep cavity of sand beneath a driftwood log bordering the pond.

On Monday, forty-eight hours after his release, Chuck Geschke once again entered the Adobe parking lot, this time escorted to his office door by a phalanx of FBI agents and bodyguards. He and Nan gave an emotional first-person account of their ordeal to all Adobe employees called together in two sessions in the company cafeteria.

After publicly thanking family, friends, and the FBI for their roles in his rescue, Chuck promised his coworkers that he was unhurt and promised that the employees and the company were as safe and secure as always. His physical presence, however, seemed to be the best reassurance for the scores of stunned, shaken, and tearful employees who lined up for hugs and handshakes with the Geschke family.

The following day, the family left for the security and anonymity of Nantucket Island, stopping first in an airline conference room at the Newark airport for an emotional reunion with their shocked and incredulous son and brother, John. Every detail of each one's personal story of the last five days was unraveled for John until the pain of his exclusion and distance slowly began to ease.

Mouhannad "Steve" Albukhari, twenty-six, a Syrian-born U.S. citizen, was arrested by the FBI for the abduction of Charles Geschke following his interrogation in Marina. His twenty-three-year-old accomplice, Ahmad Mohammed "Rock" Sayeh, a Jordanian who had entered the United States on a student visa in 1987, was arrested by the FBI as he fled the Hodel Court house shortly before the FBI raid.

Albukhari quickly pled guilty and, less than six months after the crime, was sentenced to prison for life plus twenty years, with a possibility of parole. He is now serving his term in the Avenal State Prison in Avenal, California.

After a jury trial in 1994, Sayeh was convicted of kidnapping, robbery, and making terrorist threats. Like Albukari, he was sentenced to life with possible parole and was incarcerated at Mule Creek State Prison in Ione, California. In August of 2010, Sayeh was granted parole and deported to his native country of Jordan the following October. Since he was convicted of a crime while living in this country on a visa, deportation was required by law as a condition of parole.

After thorough investigation of Chuck's "third man" report, the FBI determined that Sayeh had changed his shoes and altered his voice to fortify the impression of an organization behind the crime. Chuck supported this conclusion since, several days after his rescue, he remembered that the "third man's" Nike running shoes glimpsed from beneath his blindfold were exactly the same as the shoes he had seen on Rock's feet early in the week of his captivity.

Afterword
2010

Chuck

Chuck Geschke, now seventy-one, is living an active life as a retiree in both Los Altos and Nantucket Island. He plays golf, travels widely, and still co-chairs the board of Adobe Systems along with his partner and friend, John Warnock. Chuck also serves as advisor or board member to several community, arts, and education organizations. He and Nan speak regularly to civic and church groups about the kidnapping experience and the insights it gave them into the meaning of life.

Q. Why did you decide to write your story now, after so many years?

A. A couple of reasons. First of all, it took a long time to resolve all the conflict and emotion I felt and then to process what really happened. In the beginning, I had no desire at all to relive what had happened. I wanted to put it behind us, go on with life the way it was. I probably repressed a lot of my feelings in those first few years so I could appear strong and "normal" to my family. But gradually, Nan and I were invited to speak at local events about the kidnapping and how we coped with the stress and terror. That made us examine things more closely. Those speeches were the real impetus to tell our story more publicly. So many people would come up to us afterward to say how our story gave them courage to carry on through some trouble or pain in their lives. That was incredibly satisfying. We began to believe our experience might help people cope with traumatic life events—like grief, violence, addiction, and so on. That's why we wrote the book.

Q. *What would you say is the most important thing you learned from your experience that would be helpful to others?*

A. The key impact for me? No question. I realized in a way I never had before the incredible importance of my belief in God and a providential spirit. Ultimately that's what allowed me to get through this and return to a life without hatred or bitterness. The other major lesson, I think, was recognizing that my love for my family was fundamental to everything I did in my life. In this case, I knew my family was in crisis and that I would do anything to protect them. So I had a fierce will to survive—for them.

Q. *Have you changed as a result of your experience?*

A. In one way, maybe. I always used to keep a careful wall between my secular and spiritual life. Now there's a crack. I am more comfortable talking about my faith—not in an evangelizing way, but in an affirming way, acknowledging its importance in my life. It's now part of my public personality, not just my private side. As for other fundamental changes, no. Nan and I are still a couple of runny-nosed kids from Cleveland, Ohio. Most of our longtime friends would say that's true.

Because of the kidnapping, I was exposed to diverse groups of people who have all enriched my life. The FBI, for example; the legal community; the justice system; all the people who have told us that our story has helped them cope with bad experiences of their own. So I think I became better educated, more appreciative, and more sensitive in many ways. Still, it was too high a price to pay. I'd rather get the same benefits in other ways.

Q. *Did your faith or relationship with God change after the kidnapping?*

A. Not fundamentally, though gratitude is a larger part of my prayer life. I never see my wife and three children, their spouses, and our seven grandchildren gathered around the table when I'm not overwhelmed with gratitude that I am there with them. That feeling never goes away. I'd say God has a slightly different place in my life, because I think more about what he expects of me. When you've faced certain death and then been given another chance at life, you wonder what you're being asked to do for your remaining time on earth. How can I have a more positive impact? I have a definite sense of mission now.

Q. *Are you saying that your faith in God rescued you?*

A. Not in the literal sense, no. But my belief in a personal God, my comfort level in "talking" to God, praying to him, and asking for help gave me great comfort and support. I felt less alone. And all of this is a part of hope. I was blessed with hope almost all the way through.

Q. *Is faith in God the reason you were able to endure and overcome this terrible stress in your life while many cannot?*

A. I don't know if it comes from faith or not, but I believe most people have innate strength they aren't aware of; they just need to discover it and develop it. Faith, or a strong belief system, helps. Strong parents help. I was extremely lucky in the parenting department. My parents were nurturing and supportive and had an unshakeable commitment to their Catholic faith, so my belief system was constantly reinforced by them and later by my teachers in Catholic schools—mostly Jesuit priests.

Q. *What about people who don't have supportive families or even a belief in God? People who grow up with all kinds of disadvantages. How do they develop their inner strength?*

A. I won't deny it's more difficult to delve into your soul and find personal power without a religion or a strong, loving family. But people do it all the time, primarily by finding good role models. We hear all about role models for business success. Why not for personal and spiritual success? I'd say find people you admire for reasons other than financial or social success. People who are calm and balanced and goal-directed in their personal lives, even when bad things happen to them. If you fill your life with good people, good influences, and sound principles, you become more skilled at controlling your reactions in the face of disappointment or disaster. Sure you still get scared and sad and worried at times, but you won't let those circumstances control your life and change who you are. That's inner strength.

Q. *What advice do you have for people who can't practice for a crisis because they are in the midst of one right now? Sudden painful circumstances such as the loss of a child, spousal violence, a diagnosis of cancer, or some other catastrophe?*

A. I learned that we need to seek support outside ourselves when we're hurting or afraid. It's sometimes very hard to accept the generosity of others, but it can be healing, too. Let other people do things for you, depend on others. Express your anxieties to a good friend or two. The process of talking itself gives you good insights. Relationships with others give you strength and purpose. We're social beings, and we need connection. I'm convinced we're all here to help one another. People really *want* to help one another. So, accept and acknowledge that you're in the midst of a painful time and depend on others. If it hadn't been for my absolute trust in my family's love and my friends' loyalty, I wouldn't have had much hope.

Q. *Was there ever a time that you abandoned hope?*

A. The lowest point of the five days came very early Saturday morning, probably around 5:00 AM, when I tried to escape and was recaptured. I had seen my briefcase with my initials scratched into it saying "CG is dead." And now I had seen the second kidnapper's face. At point I felt it was all over, that I would be killed whether they got the money or not. It was a definite turning point in my attitude and the way I prayed. Not exactly a loss of hope, but more a total surrender to God's will. I accepted that I was no longer in control, and after that I felt peaceful—still scared out of my mind, but inwardly calm. I put myself completely in God's hands and trusted in his plan for me. I think this acceptance was the key to avoiding true despair.

Q. *If that was your lowest point, was there a high point? Given the circumstances, maybe it should be called "the most hopeful point."*

A. That's easy. It was when the first kidnapper came back from a phone call irritated that Kathy was trying to negotiate with him. My heart just exploded with pride and love. It was such a powerful connection with my family. It proved that they were being smart and brave, and it gave me enormous hope that everything could still turn out okay.

Q. *A couple of times during your imprisonment, you managed to see some humor. How did you manage to recognize humor when you were so tense and fearful?*

A. I always felt those few, odd moments when something seemed funny were a special grace sent to help break the tension. Kind of like the sudden urge to laugh during a funeral. It was probably a defense mechanism to save me from going over the edge! I've always had a cynical type of humor that sees the ironies in daily life. In fact, I often use humor in business situations to defuse conflict and disagreements. In this situation, though, the fear always came charging back.

Q. *Speaking of business, did your skills as a manager and executive help you out in any way during your captivity?*

A. Yes, absolutely. Whether it was wise or not, I tried to negotiate with the kidnappers for certain concessions on the night of the money drop—like not having Kathy walk onto the beach alone. I tried to create some mistrust between the two by suggesting to Rock that Steve might be planning to take off by himself with all the money. I talked them into letting me read the daily headline on the recorded message so I could at least let my family know I was still alive. This is the kind of strategic thinking that's second nature in corporate life. These small victories gave me hope because I felt some measure of control, miniscule though it was.

Q. *How did your Adobe coworkers react when they learned of your abduction?*

A. Only a handful of employees knew from the beginning what had happened. Though the FBI had been in and out, combing my office and files for clues and talking to some of the management team, they wanted to keep everything under wraps until they knew what they were dealing with. They were adamant about keeping the media out until they knew I was safe, for which I am still grateful. That alone could have saved my life. The first story ran in the San Jose paper on Sunday morning, but many people still didn't know what had happened until Monday, when Nan and I called an all-employee meeting in the cafeteria and explained where I had been for the past week. I'd say the company was shocked. Several were frightened and tearful on my behalf, which warmed my heart.

Q. *Are there any long-term effects? Anything you're still dealing with as a result of the experience?*

A. Yes. After all these years, I still have trouble sleeping and can easily fall into a depressive state where I find it hard to focus or read. I'm told it's probably the remains of post-traumatic stress syndrome. I have medication to help with those issues. And certain random events can still trigger suspicion and anxiety. In the short term, we all had counseling for several months, and I also think leaving town right after it happened helped tremendously.

Q. Do you feel completely safe today?

A. I'd say yes. But it took a couple of years for me to stop looking over my shoulder each time I entered a parking lot or got on an elevator. At first, the FBI provided bodyguards for all of us, but once we landed in Nantucket, we felt anonymous and safe enough to give up the personal protection. Allowing myself to feel safe again was a gradual process. For example, Nan and I were in Paris a couple of years after the kidnapping and someone snatched her purse in a metro station. On a different trip, a Middle Eastern man, a pickpocket, jostled against me on an escalator in an attempt to get my wallet. Both occasions made me very angry and fearful and negative. Even now, I'll become unusually suspicious if I see a strange car in the neighborhood, for instance. For the first few months, unexpected loud noises would make me shake and shiver uncontrollably. But that was temporary.

Q. Why was the trip to Nantucket so important to you?

A. It helped to get us back in balance as a family. For me, there was an overwhelming sense of gratitude that we were all together. Other than my dad and Diane, there were no relatives with us. Just the nuclear family without the distractions of our personal or business lives. We talked and fished and played together. I remember pitching balls, playing cards and board games. Lots of laughing and, I guess you'd say, a kind of clinging together. I didn't talk much about the kidnapping after we all shared our stories with John. It was definitely there in the background, but a lot of the tension dropped away when we landed on the island. Looking back, we were probably repressing the fact that such a terrible thing happened, because it was so important to all of us to carry on with our lives as they were. We were determined not to let the experience continue to terrorize us. I refused to live in fear or let my family live in fear. The biggest change in the family was that we gained a new appreciation of one another.

• • •

Nan

Nan Geschke, sixty-eight, continues to be a community leader in both Los Altos and Nantucket, especially through her service to their historical commissions and libraries. During her corporate years, she served as president of the Special Libraries Association and later developed a popular television series on Los Altos history. She and Chuck travel often and enjoy regular gatherings and vacations with their children and grandchildren.

Q. *Looking back on the kidnapping experience from the perspective of almost twenty years, what is the most significant impression you were left with?*

A. The one thing I understood with striking clarity after this experience is that the trivialities of life are not important when a life is at stake. To put it another way, all the things we plan for and think about and worry about day after day become trivial. They simply drop away in the immediacy of the situation before you. Nothing has value but the life or lives in jeopardy.

Q. *How did you use this revelation to improve or change your life?*

A. I think I began to value my own life more, to see it as a gift, and to ask myself how much of this gift I was sharing with others. After the kidnapping, I felt a greater need to be committed to something outside myself. To me, getting Chuck's life back, getting our family life back meant there was an obligation to return something. There was—and still is—a sense of being spared for some purpose or some mission. Because of that feeling, I view time differently. I believe that God, my family, and the people I work with all have a right to expect the best use of my time. I owe them the best of me. What I'm saying overall is that there's a terrific sense of obligation along with the gratitude. That wasn't always so before this event.

Q. *Did your family life change after the kidnapping?*

A. As you would expect, there was a natural progression of changes in our family as the children developed careers, got married, and so on. But to this day, we all go to great lengths to keep our family cohesive. We take two vacations together every year, we gather for every holiday, and we manage our family foundation together. We definitely value one another more, but with all the different family and work and school schedules, it takes a lot of effort to get together. Family has to be a conscious priority. But because everyone works to make it happen, the constant underlying message to one another is, "You are important to me."

Q. *Why do you think your family was able to come through this trauma even closer, while so many families are torn apart under extreme stress?*

A. Some of the circumstances were in our favor. For one thing, we had the extremes of stress for a relatively short time span, though it *felt* endless. And while the trial was awful to get through and didn't take place until two years later, we still didn't have to live with the trial uncertainty for years and years like some people do. It helped that one of the criminals pleaded guilty and that there was so much concrete evidence against both of them. The other important thing was that our family made a commitment to one another to work through it together. Many people expected us to retreat, to have bodyguards and fancy security systems. But we saw that as giving a victory to crime. We were determined *not* to let this experience ruin us as a family. We all agreed to counseling, which gave us help to talk through our emotions.

Q. *At various times, everyone has mentioned that the trip to Nantucket was an important healing time for your family. Was that so for you?*

A. I can't emphasize enough how important that trip was. In my opinion, it was the key element in coping with the immediate aftereffects, specially for me. For a while, I tried to cope by shutting out reality. I shut Chuck out, didn't want to talk about it, sort of let days go by in a blur. It was really hard for Chuck to cope with his issues and try to deal with mine, too. But the island worked its magic on us. The trip was providential. It made me very aware of the hand of God in our healing process. We felt so safe, so much at home that it just seemed natural for us to start looking for a home there. When we found some property and decided to build a house, we were all suddenly involved in a positive, exciting project—together. To this day, that house belongs equally to every one of us. To any family suffering the aftereffects of a tragedy or trauma, I would recommend a family project where everyone participates and everyone contributes. Nothing is more therapeutic.

Q. *You and Chuck both say that your faith is the inner strength that allowed you to survive this ordeal. How did your faith help you to cope?*

A. First of all, my faith gave me a place to turn when my human strength and skill failed. I knew I was dealing with something beyond my capacity to handle on my own. All my life, when I was in a dangerous or desperate situation, my instant response was to turn to prayer. Throughout the kidnapping ordeal, my belief in a personal God who I could communicate with was critical in keeping me grounded. Believing that there is something beyond life on earth, that we have a soul, that there is life after death—all these convictions help to put suffering in perspective. That knowledge doesn't take away pain or fear or anger, but it does provide an intellectual and emotional foothold for coping.

For instance, while I was pleading with God to rescue Chuck, I felt the presence and support of "the communion of saints," which Catholics and several other religions believe is the spiritual union of all the souls in heaven and on earth. I often prayed specifically to my mother, my grandmother, my aunt, and others I was close to during their lives. I asked for their protection, and I felt less alone. I was still frustrated with God, but at least I felt he heard my confusion. I couldn't understand the point of the suffering and kept asking him to show me his will in all of this.

Q. *How do you develop such a resource?*
A. I just spoke of life as a gift. Faith is, too. But, true, it has to be nourished if it's going to sustain you. I was incredibly lucky to have strong influences and examples of faith in my childhood and youth. I had a large Irish Catholic family for whom the Mass and the parish were a central part of daily life. And, I had a Catholic education from elementary school through college. I was brought up to turn to prayer, to see God's hand in everything; it's who I am. I believe that parents can give their children no greater gift than a grounding in faith. Of course, it's up to the child to accept it and develop it in his or her adult life.

And you can't forget the importance of the relationships in your life, either. Whether you call it faith or not, our experience of God comes through other people. The human connection is tremendously important in coping with tragedy and grief. Our experience is proof of that.

Q. *John and Marva Warnock have been trusted friends of your family for many years. How important was that relationship during the time of Chuck's captivity?*
A. The Warnocks are a perfect example of what I mean about having people you love and trust surround you in times of need. I completely trusted in their judgment and their loyalty to us and

would have been lost without them. Marva had a slight degree of distance from the situation, which gave her a perspective we all needed. She was the one who convinced both John and me to involve the police and FBI right away. She also got the children there quickly, took care of food for everyone, kept our friends at bay— all the things I couldn't do. Fright and confusion made me practically helpless to cope with day-to-day things like that. I will always be extremely grateful to her.

Q. *Your family describes you as a strong and decisive person, yet you took a backseat role throughout the ordeal at home. Why?*

A. I had held it together pretty well throughout Tuesday when I felt the whole thing was on my shoulders. I even threw out the FBI at one point, as my family loves to remind me! So, no, I was not as fragile as people thought, but my levels of stress and anxiety were so high that I was glad to give control to the FBI. I didn't want to take any chance that the stress might overwhelm me. I had to trust in the process, and by that time I believed that the FBI was our best and only shot at getting Chuck out of this. And once Mary Ellen O'Toole took over the operation at the house, Peter and Kathy and I all felt totally safe and comfortable. She conveyed a remarkable mix of power and reassurance.

Q. *You were terrorized for five days. The first day you heard threats against Chuck's life and your own. The kidnapper said if you didn't cooperate he would "cut him [Chuck] up in little pieces and feed him to the sharks." Is it possible to grow or learn anything from such a cruel experience?*

A. Yes, most definitely—though the understanding comes only after you get some distance from the actual event and have time to reflect. For one thing, I learned how vital my faith was in becoming the person I am. I also believe that the strong emphasis on responsibility, in both my family and school, helped me to avoid self-pity and focus on action. I felt solely responsible for Chuck's life, especially on Tuesday, and was determined to do whatever the kidnapper asked—no matter what the cost—to save him. I think Kathy felt the same weight of responsibility. We drew courage from our sense of obligation to one another, which goes back to the importance of close relationships.

Something I learned about myself was that I tend to pull away, to retreat from others when I'm hurting emotionally. But the extreme danger and desperation of the kidnapping situation forced me to rely on so many others for support. I learned how important it is to allow people to minister to you when you're in need. It's not always easy since we're so programmed to be independent—but what a valuable lesson!

Q. *What convinced you that the caller's threats were real?*

A. Well, as I said, Chuck was uncharacteristically out of touch that morning, so that was one clue. I was also aware of the Sidney Reso executive kidnapping that had been in the news that month. And there had been some terrorist activity in California in the past year. In fact, my first thought was that a terrorist group was holding Chuck. All this flashed through my mind and made the call seem credible.

Q. *How did you feel about Kathy's taking on the role of negotiator?*

A. Worried, scared, anxious. She was so young to be put in such a risky, desperate position. But I didn't argue with the FBI. They were the experts.

Q. *Did you have any physical reactions to all the stress?*

A. I remember a couple of things. In the first thirty seconds of the phone call from the kidnapper on Tuesday, I was completely confused. Then, when it clicked that Chuck was missing from his office and that this could be real, I literally went cold. It was like a freezing wind swept through my entire body. Later, every time I remembered that I almost slammed the phone down thinking it was a crank call, or that I was about to leave the house and almost missed the call, the same experience of freezing would come over me.

The other thing was my reaction to the telephone ringing. It was set extremely loud so no call would be missed. Every time it rang it would jar the whole house, and my heart rate would shoot way up. I'd start praying for Kathy, and when she raised her voice a few times, my heart would start speeding and hammering again. There was terror in just knowing that the kidnapper was on the phone. Then for a couple of years afterward, I'd get sudden anxiety attacks for no apparent reason. I'd have trouble catching my breath, I'd hyperventilate. Those things resolved themselves over time.

Q. *Were there psychological repercussions? Any long-term effects?*
A. We were lucky in that we were surrounded by people we trusted: our friends, the Adobe employees, people who worked for us around the house. Our trust in them kept us from feeling threatened. Our trust in God's plan for us helped, too. Still, I had periods of insomnia triggered by worry and stress, and Chuck still has occasional nightmares. I guess you could say we both have ongoing sleep issues, though by now we have learned how to cope with them.

Q. *What do you hope this book will accomplish?*
A. One goal was simply to have this record for our family archives. Another personal goal was to provide an organized way to process the experience as a family. We've learned about and understood one another's feelings in ways we had never done before. But the real reason was the growing and nagging feeling that our experience might be of some service to other people. If our story helps someone gain perspective or hope or peace in coping with

some trauma, it will be worth it. In fact, we feel an obligation to offer this support if we can.

• • •

Kathy

Kathy Geschke Orciuoli, now forty-three, is an interior designer. She and her husband have two small boys and live in Menlo Park, about thirty minutes from her parents' Los Altos home.

Q. *At the time of your father's kidnapping, you were only twenty-four years old, yet you became the central figure in negotiating for his release. Did that role surprise or upset you?*

A. It wasn't surprising that my dad prepared the kidnappers for the possibility of talking to me. He liked to tell our family and friends that I was the only one who could get us off a deserted island if we were stranded. He also knew my mom was totally exhausted after the Russia trip and that the stress might be too much for her. I wouldn't ordinarily step in for my mom, but we all knew, including Mom, that she was on shaky ground in high-anxiety situations—and this was the most extreme anxiety any of us ever experienced. So if the FBI believed I was the best chance for my dad's safe recovery, I would obviously do everything in my power to cooperate. But was I upset? Yes. Scared to death.

Q. *You formed an extraordinary bond with Special Agent Mary Ellen O'Toole, the criminal profiler who prepared you and debriefed you for each phone call. Will you describe the relationship you and she developed during the four days she was with you?*

A. Mary Ellen and I did become very close. She is an incredible person, and I've never known anyone like her before or since. She had such tremendous faith in me. She made me feel that we were doing every single thing we could to get my dad back safely, and I never once doubted her. She must have sensed from the beginning that I could be aggressive when I wanted something and that I had a tendency to take charge of situations. She built that confidence in me, and I trusted her completely. She was so matter-of-fact, so decisive, and so smart. She never sugarcoated the truth. Yet she was very tender and kind. All of us, even the other agents, leaned on her. She was my rock.

Q. *Even though Mary Ellen guided you through the phone calls, you were still talking with someone who had threatened to kill you and your family. What did that feel like?*

A. I was terrified. It was unbelievably stressful because I had to accomplish so many things on each phone call. Mary Ellen gave me questions and key phrases that would help her assess the kidnapper's level of intelligence and experience. Other agents wanted me to concentrate on the voice to see if I could identify it. The thought that I might know the person doing this to my family turned my stomach. Mary Ellen would pat my back continuously to give me courage and confidence.

I remember a few times almost dropping to the floor during or right after the calls. Afterward, I would be shaking, very nervous about how I did or whether I could have done something more or better that would have helped find my dad faster. It felt like a terrible burden on my shoulders. The FBI would then analyze every word and tone of voice in order to set the strategy for the next call. They worked with my brother to type up the new scripts and guidelines for me.

Q. *Your mother and Peter often prayed the Rosary—especially when you were taking the phone calls. Do you think their prayers helped you?*

A. I loved knowing that they were praying for me. It was comforting to know that they were asking God to watch over me. It also made me feel stronger, more determined.

Q. *Did you pray?*
A. I don't remember praying. Maybe I prayed unconsciously in my head or a couple of times with Mom and Pete. I was so focused on staying strong for my dad and mom that I didn't have time or thoughts for anything else—even God. It seemed like my only job was to keep our family together. Their safety was up to me. I was very, very tense and scared, and I knew I *needed* prayers. Thank God they were doing it for me!

Q. *Did you feel that God had abandoned you or your family at any point? Were you angry?*
A. Angry at God? Yes, definitely. I could not imagine why our family was being put through such hell—especially after the shooting death of Mom's sister, my aunt Kathy. That was so hard on my mom, and she was just coming out of it. I felt God was being unfair to us. I learned later that this kind of anger is one of the natural stages of grief.

Q. *When your brother John called, you sensed he was suspicious of your explanations of why neither of your parents could speak with him. You also worried about deceiving your grandfather. What effect did the deception have on you?*
A. It was really difficult and made me feel awful. But we couldn't risk having John drill Mom for answers, and if Pete had answered the phone at our house on a weekday, John would've known for sure something was very wrong. He even thought it was odd for me to be there. I just kept telling him how sick everyone was and how I was there to help out. We would send regular faxes to my grandfather with the same message. He was used to a daily call or visit

from one of us, so not seeing us for five days probably worried him. I had to keep telling myself that it was right not to involve them, that they were safer that way. With John on the East Coast and Grandpa being ninety-one years old, there was absolutely nothing either of them could have done to help us.

Q. *You had to deceive your friends, too, didn't you?*

A. That was even harder, I think, because I was behaving so out of character. I missed several graduation parties, a long-planned girls' day at the spa, and just the normal evenings out with my friends. I would usually speak to several of my friends daily, and it was so hard not to pick up the phone and let them know about the hell my family was going through. They would call, and I would say no to everything they wanted me to do, trying my best to sound convincing, but failing miserably, I'm sure. Several of my friends got very worried about me, and one even asked if I was being held against my will. What irony! If I could have told them what was happening and felt their love and support and prayers, it would have definitely given me more strength.

Q. *So your brother Peter was the only person your age you could talk to?*

A. Peter and I became very close that week. He managed all the details at the house so I could focus on working with the FBI. He just seemed to understand whatever needed to be done. He was so supportive and encouraging to both Mom and me. He also knew when to distract Mom or me with a touch of humor or some kind of diversion. I don't think he'll ever know how much it meant. He was another rock for me.

Q. *On Friday evening, watching you dress in a bulletproof vest seems to have been painful for everyone—even the FBI agents. How did you feel about it? Is that when you first confronted the*

210

possible danger to yourself?

A. To answer the last question first, yes. That was when the magnitude of my situation really hit home. My sense of danger and fear was magnified a thousand times, and seeing Mom and Pete and the Warnocks struggling not to cry didn't help. So I tried to think only of my dad and how the situation would be more terrifying for him than for me. That helped a little. Knowing that I was driving into so much danger that I had to be protected by a bulletproof vest and armed guards still gives me chills.

Q. *The long drive to the drop site was a roller coaster ride for your emotions. You were pushed and pulled between terror and hope, between resentment and nostalgia, between life and death. How did that affect you?*

A. That drive was the most intense experience of my life. Knowing that my father's life depended on my doing this was absolutely terrifying. My heart was racing so fast I can't believe I actually survived it. Being surrounded by the FBI, the police, and the military was comfort in one sense but was frightening in itself. I always knew I was brave, but that night really tested my limits. Still, the whole experience taught me that I was strong, that I had the ability to survive tremendous pain and move beyond it. My husband and I have suffered many miscarriages, and I know the personal strength I gained from the kidnapping experience helped me to get through this terrible grief in my later life.

Q. *Would you say the drive to make the drop was the lowest point in the five days for you?*

A. Oddly enough, that was the most hopeful point, even though I was shaking, crying, hyperventilating, and overall scared to death. There was a sort of elation once we made the exchange. The moment I tossed that bag out of the car, I truly believed everything was over, that my dad was as good as free. I got home from the drop about 1:30 AM and had a great feeling of relief. But when hour after hour went by with no news, I was convinced something had gone wrong. The lowest point came about five or six o'clock Saturday morning when we still had not heard anything from Dad. I believed he was dead. I kept thinking: if only I had driven faster, if only we hadn't called the FBI, if only we hadn't bugged the money. I couldn't stop these thoughts. It was awful.

Q. *Do you behave differently in any ways as a result of this experience?*

A. Oh, I definitely think so. For instance, I always have my radar up. I'm much more alert to what's going on around me in any public situation, and I'm probably a little paranoid about leaving my children with other people. I have some trust issues in new situations with new people, too. Something happened a year or so after the kidnapping that made me realize how deep and permanent my level of fear is. A man attempted to hijack my car in San Francisco. Seeing a face at my car window with a gun pointed at me practically put me over the top. It brought everything back: the panic, the terror, the racing heart. Somehow I had enough thought process to floor the accelerator to try to get away. The guy hung onto the car door for more than a mile. It was the *second* most frightening experience of my life and certainly didn't help me resolve any trust or fear issues.

Q. *How did you cope with those issues?*

A. All of us had counseling, and I continued with a therapist for two years afterward, longer than the others. I tended to want to pull back from people at that time, even my friends. I preferred to be alone much more than ever before. The psychologists really encouraged me to stay very socially involved and to interact with people as much as possible. I see now that that this was to keep my fears and distrust from overtaking me. For a while, I could easily have become a recluse!

Q. Did you learn anything else about yourself?

A. Yes. I now acknowledge and respect my own strength. Others have told me for years that I was brave and strong and determined, but now I believe it! I know with absolute certainty that I will never run away from trouble. I have faith in my ability to handle what comes my way. If anything good came from this terrible experience, this self-knowledge is it. I also learned one other interesting thing about myself: if I'm ever called for jury duty, I could not be impartial about crimes of kidnapping, terrorizing, or depriving a person of freedom.

Q. Describe how you felt the moment you saw your dad getting out of the car the day he returned.

A. It was such an incredible moment! Seeing him step out of that car was beautiful. We all huddled together on the front lawn and cried uncontrollably with joy and relief. Our ordeal was over! I don't think anybody said anything for a while. We just hung on to each other. I remember feeling so safe and so lucky to be inside that circle of people I loved.

Q. You have said that holding a baby during the celebration of Chuck's return had a soothing, healing effect on you. Can you talk about that?

A. Yes, for some reason holding that sweet baby girl on Saturday evening had a profound effect on me. Kelsey was her name, and she was eleven or twelve months old. I think I needed the pure innocence that only a baby can provide to calm me and restore my faith in goodness and decency after the events of the week. I have never seen Kelsey since then, nor will she ever remember the part she played in my life. But her presence soothed me in a way no one else could have.

Q. Did your relationship with your father change after the kidnapping?

A. In one way, yes, it did. We were always close, but after the kidnapping we would check in with each other more often to make sure all was well. To this day, we still do that. I remember hearing that on the night Dad returned, he checked on me every half hour while I was sleeping. It seems like a continuation of that kind of concern for me. Another thing is that for years Dad sent flowers to my mom and me on the anniversary date of the kidnapping. My parents are both very supportive of my brothers and me, but ever since the kidnapping I have sensed something deeper in Dad's support. I think it's gratitude.

Q. Do you think this event had any special purpose or meaning in your life?

A. Well, as they say, everything happens for a reason. I know it's trite, but I really do believe that. I think the purpose for me was to show that there is no greater gift in life than a loving family and that every single day is precious. Our whole family is now more appreciative of small things. We make the most of every occasion. Every milestone in our lives or the children's lives is more joyful. We celebrate more. And I'm also more aware of an obligation to give back some of the gifts I've been given. My parents especially model that for us. I've witnessed a tremendous giving back to their community on so many levels. I'm very moved by that and very proud of them. I hope my husband and I will be the same way.

• • •

Peter

Peter Geschke, forty-five, his wife Diane, and their three sons live in Fremont, a Silicon Valley community about thirty minutes from Los Altos. A teacher at the time of the kidnapping, Peter is still an educator and now teaches advanced placement chemistry and physics to high school students.

Q. *You played an important role for your mother and sister during the five-day ordeal. Can you comment on that?*

A. I was more or less the stabilizer, the background support for both of them. And for the FBI to a lesser extent. When I got to the house on Wednesday morning, I didn't know what to expect. I remember that the lights were turned very low and everything seemed too calm, unnatural. The tension in the air was so thick you could slice it. When I talked to my mom, I realized the FBI was keeping things as quiet and orderly as possible to help minimize our fear and stress. She looked rough—hadn't slept, hadn't eaten, was scared to death, agitated, confused. Understandably.

Since I was the first of the kids to get there, I think Mom relaxed a little and felt some comfort. I guess you could say I'm the tenderhearted one—sensitive, like my mom. But when Mom and the FBI filled me in on the details, I was the one who got agitated and edgy for a while. For Kathy, I was more of a cheerleader. I tried to give her nothing but praise and encouragement. For the FBI, I was an instant resource for Dad's business contacts, bank accounts, logistics, typing the scripts for Kathy, things like that. I think everyone relied on me to hold things together, to be the family mediator. I was the go-to guy in the background.

Q. *Did you ever feel sidelined by the FBI or resent that Kathy was chosen to play "the hero"?*

A. No, not at all. The FBI pegged it right. First of all, they felt a woman would be the better choice in this situation. But even so, I would have suggested that Kathy be the point person if the FBI hadn't. She's just naturally more calm and rational under pressure than any of us, except for Dad. I don't handle changes in direction very well, and I'm not a good negotiator. There was no thought and no time for resentment in the desperate circumstances we were faced with. I was making a contribution wherever I could, and that satisfied me.

Q. *You were required to keep your fiancée in the dark about what was going on. Was that difficult for you? For her?*

A. Luckily for us, it wasn't a big deal for a couple of reasons. First, Diane knew I'd been sick, so she wasn't surprised to get the answering machine when she called my house. And it just so happened she had started a new job that week, so she was very busy and very focused on getting settled at work. I'd call her when I was pretty sure she'd be at work. I could leave a message every day without actually talking to her. If we talked in person, she would have guessed something was wrong from my voice—I'm sure of it. So we'd both get daily messages from each other, and I let it seem accidental, like we were just calling each other at the wrong times. It was only for three days, and she was so tied up in her job that we got by with it. What I really missed was being able to confide in her and feel her love and support.

Q. *What was the most terrifying moment of the ordeal for you?*

A. It would have to be early Saturday morning. I had gone to sleep for a few hours after Kathy got back from the money drop. Everyone was pretty positive that all we had to do was wait for Dad to call and tell us where he was, right? We hung on to that hope for a few hours, and I slept. But when I woke up and we still didn't have Dad, or even a word about what was happening, I lost it. I was convinced it was all over and that Dad was dead. I remember lying on the floor and moaning. I felt like a shell of myself. I was physically and emotionally miserable and ready to give up.

Q. *Your parents credit their faith and habits of prayer with giving them strength to survive. Is it the same for you?*

A. My parents are deeply committed to their faith, and they made sure all of us children got a strong foundation in our religion, which I appreciate. I hope I'm doing the same for my children. You need an anchor in your life. A belief system centers a person. I know from experience that it can help in making decisions, especially in ethics and morals.

During the kidnapping episode, it was natural for me to call on God. Mom and I prayed the Rosary a lot. The repetitive prayers helped me get to sleep. I also noticed that my conversations with God increased as the circumstances got more frightening and desperate—when I recognized that I didn't have any control.

Q. *Many families are unable to remain unified after the stress of a catastrophe or great trauma. Why do you think your family was able to recover?*

A. The FBI told us that extreme stress like this often breaks up marriages and families. I'm not sure if any one thing allowed us to get through it, but I do remember some family "rules" that my parents insisted on when we were growing up that might have made a difference in us. Like having family dinner together no matter what. Everybody would talk about their day and everybody else would listen. My parents obviously believed that we strengthened the family through this kind of communication. It wasn't always easy to find the time, and it wasn't always pleasant, either. But we learned about each other and from each other through this ritual. I think those bonds built over years and years kept us acting as a unit through this crisis.

Q. *Did your family dynamic change in any way as a result of what you endured?*

A. In some ways, yes. For the first year or two, we were more cautious, maybe suspicious, of certain people. For instance, my dad has always been a very fair-minded and welcoming person, and he was determined not be judgmental of Middle Easterners, but it took quite a while before he could relax completely on a street or in a store with people of that nationality.

After the fears subsided and we all returned to our individual lives, my parents made a more concerted effort to bring us all together regularly. To this day, we all have Sunday dinner together every week that they're in town. It's almost the same ritual we had as kids. Add birthdays and holidays to that, plus a family vacation every summer and Christmas, and it's pretty clear that we have stayed close. We all make the effort to stay connected. If we hadn't gone through this terrible time together, I doubt we'd be so determined about it.

Q. Did you change?

A. Sure. For the short term, I was a wreck. I returned to work the Monday after my dad came home. I know now it was too soon, but I felt a strong need to return to normal. Except life was anything but normal: I had a bodyguard in my classroom of seventh graders for the remainder of the school year—about ten days. For the first couple of days, I had heart palpitations, dry mouth, and would find myself literally shaking at times. I had trouble following my lesson plans and felt I couldn't teach properly. This faded away while Diane and I were in Nantucket with the family. But when we returned, I had some level of paranoia for about a year. I was always on "terror alert." Then I simply decided I couldn't live that way and worked hard to let it go. I think I'll always have a heightened level of suspicion about certain things, though.

Q. Were you angry? Are you still?

A. Until Dad was safe, I was too worried and scared to be angry. But as soon as he was returned, I was furious. I wanted violent retribution. Not death; suffering. I'm not proud to admit that at first I wanted the kidnappers to hurt, to suffer like we did. I wasn't very rational in the first few days afterward. Even for the first two years, I would get very angry very quickly over minor things—a road-rage type of anger. I was told that was a normal psychological reaction. I don't have those feelings anymore. The kidnappers are serving life terms, which I think is appropriate punishment.

• • •

John

Now forty years old, John Geschke practices law in Palo Alto, California. John; his wife, Denise; and their son and daughter live in Los Altos, less than ten minutes from his parents' University Avenue home.

Q. *In many ways, you have the most interesting perspective on the drama that played out in your family in 1992 because all of your awareness and emotion occurred after the fact. How did you first hear of your father's abduction and rescue?*

A. Ironically, I had been celebrating that whole week. Finals were just over and some of my friends and I went camping and rafting in the woods—as far away from school and civilization as we could get. After I called home on Wednesday, we didn't call a soul for four days. When I returned on Sunday—the day after my dad was rescued—there were messages all over my door to call home. My roommates were only told that I shouldn't worry but that I should call immediately. Naturally I was panicky. When I reached my parents, I simply couldn't believe what had happened to them. I was relieved my dad was okay, but I felt an overwhelming guilt that I wasn't there, that I didn't know, that I was doing crazy, adolescent stuff with my friends while my family was suffering and afraid. I still feel some of that guilt.

Q. When did you first see your family after the kidnapping?

A. Well, they were all planning to come for my graduation on June 9, which would have been two weeks to the day after my dad was kidnapped, and then we were going on to Nantucket Island for a family vacation. But after all this happened, they wanted to leave Los Altos right away. I think they wanted to put the whole incident behind them and go somewhere with no reminders. So they decided to go to Nantucket first and then come back to New Jersey for the graduation. But they wanted to see me first to give me the story first-hand, before I read or heard all the variations and interpretations of the media. So we all met privately in one of the airline club rooms at Newark airport. That was the Tuesday following the kidnapping, exactly one week later.

Q. Can you describe the meeting?

A. It was very emotional. I was shocked and surprised to see how drained and exhausted they all looked—not just Dad. But it was strange for me. I felt disconnected from my family for the first time in my life. I felt I couldn't relate to them since I wasn't a part of the experience they all shared. I wasn't a part of their "inner circle." I felt ambivalent and actually a little tense. They all told me their individual stories, almost as if it were an obligation to recount every single moment for me so I could somehow be a part of it. I was sympathetic and supportive, but at the same time I felt enormously guilty that I didn't do my part, that I didn't go through this horrible experience with everybody else.

Q. Even though you were spared the pain of the actual event, was there any impact other than guilt?

A. Oh, absolutely. Yes. The whole month of June was awful for me. It nearly killed me to watch my family deal—or not deal—with the aftereffects of being terrorized. I got very angry and confrontational at times because I believed my parents were denying the tremendous psychological fallout from all the stress. They were trying to behave as though everything was back to normal. To me, it wasn't normal at all. My mom was withdrawing into herself, pretending there was nothing to talk about, and my dad didn't bring up any of his issues in order to keep things "normal" for everybody else. I was mad at both of them! I think I was afraid our family would break or change under this kind of tension.

Q. Did this tension change your role within the family?

A. Yes—because I changed. Being an "outsider" in this whole thing, I felt I could see and understand things that my parents could not. And I said so. While my comments were often painful for my parents to hear, that month of June turned out to be a cathartic time. I felt I went from child to parent at zero to sixty. I started to see my parents as vulnerable, flawed human beings rather than just "parents." I watched them suffering, trying to cope.

The following year, when I got more distance from my emotions, I saw myself as an adult during that summer, a peer. I was actually contributing something valuable to my parents and my family. I was relating to them on a different level. Overall, the change in my relationship with my mother and father was very positive—the good resulting from the bad, if you will.

Q. Has your family changed overall?

A. Yes, in some ways, but not in the negative ways I originally feared. For the first few years after the kidnapping, we all expressed our affection for one another more. There was a greater feeling of gratitude and appreciation for each other. With Dad more than any of us, it's always apparent and always expressed, to this day. He's also more spiritual.

But there's still the same respect for the boundaries of our individual lives. We don't get involved in or make judgments on each other's business, but there's an absolute certainty that we can rely on one another in any situation—no matter what. We do a kind of dance between unity and distance in our family. We might disagree on things, but we avoid confrontations. There's an unspoken commitment to remaining close despite our politics or beliefs. There's nothing more sacred to my family than staying close.

Q. How about your dad? Other than his ongoing expressions of gratitude, what changes have you seen in him?

A. I think my dad was profoundly affected by the violation to his person and his security. He had approached these guys in the parking lot entirely open to them, friendly, offering to help them. The result was a complete reversal of the expectations most of us have. To me, Dad seems much more aware of how fragile our freedom is and how dependent we are on others to behave according to certain norms. The experience must have been a huge slap in the face to him and to his ideals.

There's another change, too. He still bends over backward not to give in to fear or paranoia. He doesn't isolate himself, he doesn't back away from people, he doesn't have any unusual security measures for himself or his property or on his travels. If I'd had the same experience, I'm sure I'd be more suspicious of everyone and I'd have a much tighter security system around me. But to him, living in a "bubble" like that would be giving in to the criminals, and I admire that aspect. My dad has more faith in God and humanity than I do!

Q. The FBI has credited your dad with thinking strategically at certain times during his captivity, despite his constant fear. They say this is very unusual. Knowing your dad, how would you have expected him to react to being threatened and terrorized?

A. It's second nature for my dad to work his way out of something mentally, so it's no surprise that he would be setting up a strategy—that's just how he's wired. His world view is "mathematical."

For instance, I can see him calculating the steps or processes that would be required for him to get free. Being scared to death not only for himself, but for the rest of us, would probably make him more cautious, but I guarantee he would be constantly structuring a plan to save everyone. I'm sure this approach contributed to saving him.

Q. *Did your views on crime or criminal justice change in the wake of your family's experience?*

A. No. Even though I was angry that my family had been victimized by a terrible crime, my faith in the criminal justice system and my belief that capital punishment is never an option have remained the same. I'm certain that my parents feel the same way. I did change my thinking on parole, though. At each parole hearing for the kidnappers, I get nervous for my dad because I know his level of fear and paranoia would increase if one or both of these criminals were paroled. (See note* on p.xii of Preface.) The feeling of personal security that he has worked so hard to regain would be compromised. He has admitted this to me.

Q. *What is the most important thing you learned from your experience with crime and fear?*

A. That I can count on my family no matter what. I hope that other people don't have to go through something so drastic to realize the importance of family closeness. In a crisis, your faith and your family are all you have. I was struck with this knowledge in the most forceful way possible—under a death threat to someone I loved. This insight will guide my life, and I'm thankful for it.

ACKNOWLEDGEMENTS

MY GRATEFUL THANKS to the following people whose support helped to make this book become a reality: the *FBI agents* who generously shared their time, memories, and files, especially *Dr. Mary Ellen O'Toole* and *Special Agents Larry Taylor, Ken Thompson, Tom LaFreniere, and Ann Todd; Linda Kennedy,* kind friend and former president of a major publishing house, whose guidance and deep knowledge of the book industry was exceptionally helpful in navigating my approach to both the narrative and the market; the unequalled Cary Writers Group: *Amanda, Belinda, Christa, Jim, Scott, Sharon—and especially Bren—*whose encouragement, professional experience, and creative insights continue to be invaluable—and to generous friend and reader, *Cindy,* for her keen editorial eye; *Mrs. Alheli Olivares* of #2 Hodel Court in Hollister, who allowed us to tour and photograph the interior of her home, which is constructed identically to #5 Hodel Court where Chuck was held; *Mark and Kathy Bagby,* present owners of 470 University Avenue in Los Altos, who also allowed us gracious access to the interior of the home where the Geschkes lived at the time of this incident; the four most faithful fans and encouraging supporters of all time: *Marty and Heather, Mimi and Tom,* along with the *grand*-est, most *un*-critical cheering section a person can have—*Maggie, Michael, William, Joey, Charlie, and Bridget* (all of whom granted me hero status for working with the FBI); and, naturally and always, my most loyal, supportive, patient, and perceptive critic, friend, and lifetime companion—my husband, *Wil.*

JO ANN HOFFMAN